SAUNDARYALAHARĪ

ॐ

श्रीचक्रम्

ŚRĪ-CAKRA (FRONTISPIECE)

The Śrī-Cakra is the yantric depiction of the Divine Mother, which is described in detail in verse 11 of the Saundaryalahrī. This is also the Yantra for verse 22. The mother is often worshipped in and through the Śrī-Cakra.

SAUNDARYALAHARĪ

OF ŚAṄKARĀCĀRYA

Sanskrit Text in Devanāgarī with Roman Transliteration, English Translation, Explanatory Notes, Yantric Diagrams and Index

V. K. SUBRAMANIAN

MOTILAL BANARSIDASS PUBLISHERS
PRIVATE LIMITED • DELHI

First Edition: Delhi, 1977
Reprint: Delhi, 1980, 1986, 1990, 1993

ISBN: 81-208-0202-0 (Cloth)
ISBN: 81-208-0208-x (Paper)

Also available at:
MOTILAL BANARSIDASS
41 U.A. Bungalow Road, Jawahar Nagar, Delhi 110 007
120 Royapettah High Road, Mylapore, Madras 600 004
16 St. Mark's Road, Bangalore 560 001
Ashok Rajpath, Patna 800 004
Chowk, Varanasi 221 001

PRINTED IN INDIA

BY JAINENDRA PRAKASH JAIN AT SHRI JAINENDRA PRESS, A-45 NARAINA INDUSTRIAL AREA, PHASE I, NEW DELHI 110 028 AND PUBLISHED BY NARENDRA PRAKASH JAIN FOR MOTILAL BANARSIDASS PUBLISHERS PVT. LTD., BUNGALOW ROAD, JAWAHAR NAGAR, DELHI 110 007

TO MY MOTHER

$6.95

CONTENTS

Page : v
DEDICATION

Pages : ix-x
PREFACE

Pages : 1-54
TEXT OF SAUNDARYALAHARĪ
Devanāgarī Version
Roman Transliteration
Explanatory Notes

Page : 55
YANTRAS OF SAUNDARYALAHARĪ

Pages : 57-106
YANTRIC DIAGRAMS OF INDIVIDUAL VERSES

Pages : 107-112
PĀDA INDEX

PREFACE

The *Saundaryalaharī* of Ādi Śaṅkarācārya is essentially a poem of intense devotion, despite the Tantric concepts contained in it. There is basically no difference between the Vedic ideals of Godhead and the Tantric. The conception of Śiva and Śakti in *Tantra* is the same as the Vedic one of *Puruṣa* and *Prakṛti* and the Advaitic *Brahman* and *Māyā*.

In the words of Vivekananda, "The Absolute is formless, but energy is female. When the energy takes form, it is called *Mother*. *Mother* is the moving Power, disturbing into waves the water-calm of the Absolute." The formless infinite becomes finite in diversified creation due to *Śakti*, the Kinetic Power. To quote Arthur Avalon, "Power implies a Power-Holder. The Power-Holder is Śiva. There is no Śiva without Śakti, or Śakti without Śiva. The Two, as they are, in themselves are one. They are each Being, Consciousness, and Bliss."

Prayer is the path of purification of the mind and aids in developing in the individual worshipper the consciousness of being one with God. Indian hymns of prayer contain elements of auto-suggestion and self-hypnotism that help the spiritual aspirant in his upward path through *Sāmīpya*, *Sārūpya* and *Sāyūjya*, that is by creating a sense of nearness to the Divine, a desire to acquire the attributes of divinity, and ultimate identification of the individual self with the Supreme.

The *Saundaryalaharī* of Śaṅkarācārya is such a potent prayer. It makes the devotee feel that he is one with Śiva and Śakti, and thus arouses the latent powers within him. The Mother of the universe is the fountain-head of beauty, riches, and knowledge. The devotee, sensing his identification with, Her, becomes the lord of riches and learning, and begets such a dazzling form that he is taken to be the god of love. And yet he does not get enmeshed in earthly bondage.

True worship is the worship in and by the mind. This is termed as *Samayā* worship. Through the *Saundaryalaharī*, probably his only Tantric work, Śrī Śaṅkara shows the pure *Samayā* way of awakening the Power that lies dormant in every one of us, as *Kuṇḍalinī-śakti*. With an awakened *Kuṇḍalinī*, one lives a full life of achievement and at its end merges joyfully in the Supreme Bliss.

In placing this edition of *Saundaryalaharī*, with English translation, Notes and Yāntric diagrams, I invite all the readers thereof to take a holy dip in this ocean of bliss and beauty, bequeathed to us by the Great Master.

V. K. SUBRAMANIAN

SIMLA,
Vijayadaśamī,
October 2, 1976

सौन्दर्यलहरी

THE SAUNDARYALAHARĪ

1

Śivaḥ śaktyā yukto yadi bhavati śaktaḥ prabhavituṁ
Na cedevaṁ devo na khalu kuśalaḥ spanditum api |
Atastvām ārādhyāṁ harihararviriñcādibhir api
Praṇantuṁ stotuṁ vā katham akṛtapuṇyaḥ prabhavati ||1||

शिवः शक्त्या युक्तो यदि भवति शक्तः प्रभवितुं
न चेदेवं देवो न खलु कुशलः स्पन्दितुमपि ।
अतस्त्वामाराध्यां हरिहरविरिञ्चादिभिरपि
प्रणन्तुं स्तोतुं वा कथमकृतपुण्यः प्रभवति ॥ १ ॥

Trans. : If the Auspicious One is united with His power, He is able to create. If He is not thus, He is not capable of stirring even. Hence how can one without virtue, prostrate or praise you, who is venerated by the three Deities of creation, protection, and destruction ?

Notes : Creation is the result of the union of Śiva and Śakti, the power-holder and power. The formless Infinite becomes the myriad forms of life through power, *śakti*.

2

Tanīyāṁsaṁ pāṁsuṁ tava caraṇapaṅkeruhabhavaṁ
Viriñciḥ saṁcinvan viracayati lokānavikalam |
Vahatyenaṁ śauriḥ katham api sahasreṇa śirasāṁ
Haraḥ saṁkṣudyainaṃ bhajati bhasitoddhūlanavidhim ||2||

तनीयांसं पांसुं तव चरणपङ्केरुहभवं
विरिञ्चिः संचिन्वन्विरचयति लोकानविकलम् ।
वहत्येनं शौरिः कथमपि सहस्रेण शिरसां
हरः संक्षुद्यैनं भजति भसितोद्धूलनविधिम् ॥ २ ॥

Trans. : Gathering a tiny speck of dust from your feet the creator ever creates worlds, the protector bears them with a thousand heads, the destroyer destroying them to ashes, performs the rite of smearing his body.

Notes : The processes of creation, protection and destruction emanate from the Supreme Power.

3

Avidyānām antastimiramihiradvīpanagarī
Jaḍānāṁ caitanyastabakamakarandasrutijharī |
Daridrāṇāṁ cintāmaṇiguṇanikā janmajaladhau
Nimagnānāṁ daṁṣṭrā muraripuvarāhasya bhavati ||3||

अविद्यानामन्तस्तिमिरमिहिरद्वीपनगरी
जडानां चैतन्यस्तबकमकरन्दस्रुतिझरी ।
दरिद्राणां चिन्तामणिगुणनिका जन्मजलधौ
निमग्नानां दंष्ट्रा मुररिपुवराहस्य भवति ॥ ३ ॥

Trans. : Oh ! Gracious One, You are the Sun which dispels the darkness of the unlettered, you are the stream of consciousness for the unthinking ignorant, you are the all-giving Cintāmaṇi stone for the poor, to those drowned by the sea of births, you are the tusks of the boar (as in Viṣṇu's Varāha incarnation*).

Notes : *The mythological story is that when the earth was submerged by the turbulent waters of the oceans through the machinations of an evil demon, Viṣṇu, the Protector of the universe, took the form of a boar and rescued the earth from under the water with the tusks.

4

Tvadanyaḥ pāṇibhyām abhayavarado daivatagaṇas-
Tvamekā naivā'si prakaṭitavarābhītyabhinayā |
Bhayāt trātuṁ dātuṁ phalam api ca vāñchāsam adhikaṁ
Śaraṇye lokānāṁ tava hi caraṇāveva nipuṇau ||4||

त्वदन्यः पाणिभ्यामभयवरदो दैवतगण-
स्त्वमेका नैवाऽसि प्रकटितवराभीत्यभिनया ।
भयात्त्रातुं दातुं फलमपि च वाञ्छासमधिकं
शरण्ये लोकानां तव हि चरणावेव निपुणौ ॥ ४ ॥

Trans. : All gods other than you grant boons by their hands. You alone differ. To protect from fear and grant fruits more than desired, in all the worlds, Oh ! Refuge, Your feet alone are competent.

5

Haristvām ārādhya praṇatajanasaubhāgyajananīṁ
Purā nārī bhūtvā purāripum api kṣobham anayat |
Smaro'pi tvāṁ natvā ratinayanalehyena vapuṣā
Munīnām apyantaḥ prabhavati hi mohāya mahatām ||5||

हरिस्त्वामाराध्य प्रणतजनसौभाग्यजननीं
पुरा नारी भूत्वा पुररिपुमपि क्षोभमनयत् ।
स्मरोऽपि त्वां नत्वा रतिनयनलेह्येन वपुषा
मुनीनामप्यन्तः प्रभवति हि मोहाय महताम् ॥ ५ ॥

Trans. : Once worshipping you, who are the Mother of prosperity to those knieeling before you, Viṣnu became a woman and stirred the Supreme Ascetic the Enemy of Pura. Cupid also prostrating before you destroyed the penance of great sages dazzling them with his captivating form, the collyrium to the eyes of Rati.

Notes : The Supreme Power is the source of all beauty.

6

Dhanuḥ pauṣpaṁ maurvī madhukaramayī pañca viśikhāḥ
Vasantaḥ sāmanto malayamarudāyodhanarathaḥ |
Tathā'pyekaḥ sarvaṁ himagirisute kām api kṛpām
Apāṅgāt te labdhvā jagad idam anaṅgo vijayate ||6||

धनुः पौष्पं मौर्वी मधुकरमयी पञ्च विशिखाः
वसन्तः सामन्तो मलयमरुदायोधनरथः ।
तथाऽप्येकः सर्वं हिमगिरिसुते कामपि कृपा-
मपाङ्गात्ते लब्ध्वा जगदिदमनङ्गो विजयते ॥ ६ ॥

Trans. : Oh ! Daughter of the Himālaya mountain, obtaining a kind glance from you, Cupid conquers this world, with only his bow and five arrows of flowers, bowstring of bees, Spring as his charioteer and the Southern breeze as his chariot.

Notes : The Supreme Power is the source of all love in the world.

7

Kvaṇatkāñcīdāmā karikalabhakumbhastananatā
Parikṣīṇā madhye pariṇataśaraccandravadanā |
Dhanurbāṇān pāśaṁ sṛṇim api dadhānā karatalaiḥ
Purastād āstāṁ naḥ puramathiturāhopuruṣikā ||7||

क्वणत्काञ्चीदामा करिकलभकुम्भस्तननता
परिक्षीणा मध्ये परिणतशरच्चन्द्रवदना ।
धनुर्बाणान् पाशं सृणिमपि दधाना करतलैः
पुरस्तादास्तां नः पुरमथितुराहोपुरुषिका ॥ ७ ॥

Trans. : Let the gracious One, the pride of the Destroyer of Tripura appear before us, Her face shining like the full autumnal moon, Her body slightly bent by the weight of her pitcher-like breasts resembling the temples of the elephant, Her hands holding the bow, the arrows, the rope and the goad.

Notes : In this—and the succeeding—verse, the poet conjures up a vision of the physical image of the Divine Mother, to delight the hearts and aid the concentration of the devotees worshipping the Samaya way—in and through the mind.

8

Sudhāsindhor madhye suraviṭapivāṭīparivṛte
Maṇidvīpe nīpopavanavati cintāmaṇigṛhe |
Śivākāre mañce paramaśivaparyaṅkanilayāṁ
Bhajanti tvāṁ dhanyāḥ katicana cidānandalaharīm ||8||

सुधासिन्धोर्मध्ये सुरविटपिवाटीपरिवृते
मणिद्वीपे नीपोपवनवति चिन्तामणिगृहे ।
शिवाकारे मञ्चे परमशिवपर्यङ्कनिलयां
भजन्ति त्वां धन्याः कतिचन चिदानन्दलहरीम् ॥८॥

Trans. : A few blessed ones worship you, the Wave of Consciousness—bliss, located on the lap of the Supremely Auspicious One, on the couch of auspicious form in the residence of Cintāmaṇi, full of Kadamba trees, situated in the gem-island, surrounded by angelic trees amidst the ambrosial ocean.

9

Mahīṁ mūlādhāre kam api maṇipūre hutavahaṁ
Sthitaṁ svādhiṣṭhāne hṛdi marutam ākāśam upari |
Mano'pi bhrūmadhye sakalam api bhittvā kulapathaṁ
Sahasrāre padme saha rahasi patyā viharase ||9||

महीं मूलाधारे कमपि मणिपूरे हुतवहं
स्थितं स्वाधिष्ठाने हृदि मरुतमाकाशमुपरि ।
मनोऽपि भ्रूमध्ये सकलमपि भित्त्वा कुलपथं
सहस्रारे पद्मे सह रहसि पत्या विहरसे ॥९॥

Trans. : In the thousand-petalled lotus, *Sahasrāra*, you sport with your lord in secret, having traversed the entire path of *Kuṇḍalinī, viz.*, the element of earth in *Mūlādhāra*, water in *Maṇipūra*, fire in *Svādhiṣṭhāna*, air in *Anāhata*, ether above it in *Viśuddhi* and the mind in *Ājña* between the eye-brows.

Notes : This stanza describes the ascent of the Kuṇḍalinī Śakti. The Kuṇḍalinī Śakti exists in every one, but in varying degrees of awakening. The extent of spiritual progress is indicated by the traversing of the six psychic centres, Mūlādhāra, Maṇipūra, Svādhiṣṭhāna, Anāhata, Viśuddhi, and Ājñā by the Kuṇḍalinī, which normally sleeps dormant in the lowest centre, Mūlādhāra. Ultimate liberation is the union of Śakti with Śiva in Sahasrāra.

10

Sudhādhārāsārais caraṇayugalāntarvigalitaiḥ
Prapañcaṁ siñcantī punar api rasāmnāyamahasaḥ |
Avāpya svaṁ bhūmiṁ bhujaganibhamadhyuṣṭavalayaṁ
Svamātmānaṁ kṛtvā svapiṣi kulakuṇḍe kuhariṇi ||10||

सुधाधारासारैश्चरणयुगलान्तर्विगलितैः
प्रपञ्चं सिञ्चन्ती पुनरपि रसाम्नायमहसः ।
अवाप्य स्वां भूमिं भुजगनिभमध्युष्टवलयं
स्वमात्मानं कृत्वा स्वपिषि कुलकुण्डे कुहरिणि ॥१०॥

Trans. : Oh ! Glorious One, drenching all the veins with the nectar dripping from your feet, from the dizzy heights you descend to your abode and turning yourself into a serpentine coil sleep in the fine hole of the lotus-root-like *Mūlādhāra*.

Notes : While the previous stanza describes the ascent of the Kuṇḍalinī, the present one depicts the descent.

11

Caturbhiḥ śrīkaṇṭhaiḥ śivayuvatibhiḥ pañcabhir api
Prabhinnābhiḥ śaṁbhor navabhir api mūlaprakṛtibhiḥ |
Catuścatvāriṁśadvasudalakalāśratrivalaya-
Trirekhābhiḥ sārdhaṁ tava śaraṇakoṇāḥ pariṇatāḥ ||11||

चतुर्भिः श्रीकण्ठैः शिवयुवतिभिः पञ्चभिरपि
प्रभिन्नाभिः शंभोर्नवभिरपि मूलप्रकृतिभिः ।
चतुश्चत्वारिंशद्वसुदलकलाश्रत्रिवलय-
त्रिरेखाभिः सार्धं तव शरणकोणाः परिणताः ॥११॥

Trans. : Oh ! Supreme power, Your angles of abode become forty-four in number with four wheels of auspiciousness, five different wheels of power, nine basic roots of nature, and three encircling lines encasing eight and sixteen petals.

Notes : This is a description of Śrī-Cakra the symbolic abode of the Supreme Power.

12

Tvadīyaṁ saundaryaṁ tuhinagirikanye tulayituṁ
Kavīndrāḥ kalpante katham api viriñciprabhṛtayaḥ |
Yadālokautsukyād amaralalanā yānti manasā
Tapobhir duṣprāpām api giriśasāyujyapadavīm ||12||

त्वदीयं सौन्दर्यं तुहिनगिरिकन्ये तुलयितुं
कवीन्द्राः कल्पन्ते कथमपि विरिञ्चिप्रभृतयः ।
यदालोकौत्सुक्यादमरललना यान्ति मनसा
तपोभिर्दुष्प्रापामपि गिरिशसायुज्यपदवीम् ॥१२॥

Trans. : Oh ! Daughter of the snowy mountains, great poets like Brahmā and others are unable to describe your beauty ; anxious to see it, angelic beauties like Urvaśī and Rambhā experience in their mind the bliss of union with the Auspicious One, so difficult to attain by rigid penance.

Notes : Urvaśī and Rambhā are the classic beauties cited by poets as examples of unequalled feminine grace. The greatness of the Divine Mother's beauty is such that even Urvaśī and Rambhā, eager to see and enjoy it, want to become one with Śiva, the only One privileged to do so.

13

Naraṁ varṣīyāṁsaṁ nayanavirasaṁ narmasu jaḍaṁ
Tavāpāṅgāloke patitam anudhāvanti śataśaḥ |
Galadveṇībandhāḥ kucakalaśavisrastasicayā
Haṭhāt truṭyatkāñcyo vigalitadukūlā yuvatayaḥ ||13||

नरं वर्षीयांसं नयनविरसं नर्मसु जडं
तवापाङ्गालोके पतितमनुधावन्ति शतशः ।
गलद्वेणीबन्धाः कुचकलशविस्रस्तसिचया
हठात्त्रुट्यत्काञ्च्यो विगलितदुकूला युवतयः ॥१३॥

Trans. : Oh ! Supreme Power, hundreds of youthful women their hair-knots loosened, upper garments falling from their pot-like breasts, their girdles broken, their silken sarees slipping, pursue a decrepit ugly, old man indifferent to the art of love, on whom your kind glance has fallen.

Notes : The Supreme Power is the source of love and desire. A glance from Her can convert the most undesirable one into an object of love and desire.

14

Kṣitau ṣaṭpañcāśaddvisamadhikapañcāśadudake
Hutāśe dvāṣaṣṭiścaturadhikapañcāśadanile |
Divi dviḥṣaṭtriṁśanmanasi ca catuḥṣaṣṭir iti ye
Mayūkhāsteṣām apyupari tava pādāmbujayugam ||14||

क्षितौ षट्पञ्चाशद्द्विसमधिकपञ्चाशदुदके
हुताशे द्वाषष्टिश्चतुरधिकपञ्चाशदनिले ।
दिवि द्विःषट्त्रिंशन्मनसि च चतुःषष्टिरिति ये
मयूखास्तेषामप्युपरि तव पादाम्बुजयुगम् ॥१४॥

Trans. : Oh ! Supreme Power, the pair of your lotus-feet is above the fifty-six rays that exist in the earth-centre, fifty-two in water, sixty-two in fire, fifty-four in air, seventy-two in ether ard sixty-four in mind.

Notes : The reference here is to the six psychic centers in the human body, Mūlādhāra which represents the earth. Maṇipūra which represents the element water, Svādhiṣṭhāna fire, Anāhata air, Viśuddhi ether, and Ājñā the mind.

15

Śarajjyotśnāśuddhaṁ śaśiyutajaṭājūṭamakuṭaṁ
Varatrāsatrāṇasphaṭikaghaṭikāpustakakarām |
Sakṛnna tvā natvā katham iva satāṁ saṁnidadhate
Madhukṣīradrākṣāmadhurimadhurīṇāḥ phaṇitayaḥ ||15||

शरज्ज्योत्स्नाशुद्धां शशियुतजटाजूटमकुटां
वरत्रासत्राणस्फटिकघटिकापुस्तककराम् ।
सकृन्न त्वा नत्वा कथमिव सतां संनिदधते
मधुक्षीरद्राक्षामधुरिमधुरीणाः फणितयः ॥ १५ ॥

Trans. : Why won't words sweeter than the sweetness of honey, milk, and grapes come flooding to the good ones, after they but once prostrate before you, pure white like the autumnal moon, wearing the crescent moon and the bejewelled crown on your head, holding the book and the crystal rosary in your hands, which also grant boons and protect from fear?

Notes : In this and the two succeeding verses, the poet envisages the Goddess as the Granter of literary and artistic skills. These three verses have the Tāntric potency of conferring poetic skill.

16

Kavīndrāṇāṁ cetaḥkamalavanabālātaparuciṁ
Bhajante ye santaḥ katicidaruṇām eva bhavatīm |
Viriñcipreyasyāstaruṇataraśṛṅgāralaharī-
Gabhīrābhir vāgbhir vidadhati satāṁ rañjanam amī ||16||

कवीन्द्राणां चेतःकमलवनबालातपरुचिं
भजन्ते ये सन्तः कतिचिदरुणामेव भवतीम् ।
विरिञ्चिप्रेयस्यास्तरुणतरशृङ्गारलहरी-
गभीराभिर्वाग्भिर्विदधति सतां रञ्जनममी ॥ १६ ॥

Trans. : Those few good ones, who worship you, the Crimson One, whose effulgence, like that of the rising sun makes the lotus-clusters of great poets' minds flower, delight everyone with their profound words, flowing like the waves of youthful passion of the goddess of learning.

17

Savitrībhir vācāṁ śaśimaṇiśilābhaṅgarucibhir
Vaśinyādyābhis tvāṁ saha janani saṁcintayati yaḥ |
Sa kartā kāvyānāṁ bhavati mahatāṁ bhaṅgirucibhir
Vacobhir vāgdevīvadanakamalāmodamadhuraiḥ ||17||

सवित्रीभिर्वाचां शशिमणिशिलाभङ्गरुचिभि-
र्वशिन्याद्याभिस्त्वां सह जननि संचिन्तयति यः ।
स कर्ता काव्यानां भवति महतां भङ्गिरुचिभि-
र्वचोभिर्वाग्देवीवदनकमलामोदमधुरैः ॥ १७ ॥

Trans. : Oh! Mother, he who meditates on you, accompanied by your attendant powers like *Vaśinī* and others, the creatrices of good words, beautiful like moon-gems, becomes the creator of great works of art, using expressions fragrant like the lotus-face of the goddess of learning, resembling those of the great ones.

18

Tanucchāyābhis te taruṇataraṇiśrīsaraṇibhir
Divaṁ sarvām urvīm aruṇimani magnāṁ smarati yaḥ |
Bhavantyasya trasyadvanahariṇaśālīnanayanāḥ
Sahorvaśyā vaśyāḥ kati kati na gīrvāṇagaṇikāḥ ||18||

तनुच्छायाभिस्ते तरुणतरणिश्रीसरणिभि-
र्दिवं सर्वामुर्वीमरुणिमनि मग्नां स्मरति यः ।
भवन्त्यस्य त्रस्यद्वनहरिणशालीननयनाः
सहोर्वश्या वश्याः कति कति न गीर्वाणगणिकाः ॥१८॥

Trans. : Many celestial damsels like Urvaśī, their eyes trembling and beautiful like those of the forest does, fall under the spell of one who meditates on you bathing the heaven and earth in crimson glory, by the rays of your body, resembling the crimson rays of the rising sun.

Notes : This and the next verse have the potency of captivating women "*Striyaḥ samastāstava Devi bhedāḥ*", "All women are the facets of the Goddess", says the prayer in *Devīmāhātmya*. It is hence but natural that the devotee of the Mother finds bestowed on him the favour of all women.

19

Mukhaṁ binduṁ kṛtvā kucayugamadhas tasya tadadho
Harārdhaṁ dhyāyed yo haramahiṣi te manmathakalām |
Sa sadyaḥ saṁkṣobhaṁ nayati vanitā ityatilaghu
Trilokīm apyāśu bhramayati ravīndustanayugām ||19||

मुखं बिन्दुं कृत्वा कुचयुगमधस्तस्य तदधो
हरार्धं ध्यायेद्यो हरमहिषि ते मन्मथकलाम् ।
स सद्यः संक्षोभं नयति वनिता इत्यतिलघु
त्रिलोकीमप्याशु भ्रमयति रवीन्दुस्तनयुगाम् ॥ १९ ॥

Trans. : Oh ! Queen of the Destroyer, That he who can meditate on your *Kāmakalā* treating your face as a point, below that the pair of your breasts, and further below the womb can forthwith captivate women is an easy trifle, for such a one can quickly conquer the three worlds, whose breasts are as it were the sun and the moon.

20

Kirantīm aṅgebhyaḥ kiraṇanikurumbāmṛtarasaṁ
Hṛdi tvām ādhatte himakaraśilāmūrtim iva yaḥ |
Sa sarpāṇāṁ darpaṁ śamayati śakuntādhipa iva
Jvarapluṣṭān dṛṣṭyā sukhayati sudhādhārasirayā ||20||

किरन्तीमङ्गेभ्यः किरणनिकुरुम्बामृतरसं
हृदि त्वामाधत्ते हिमकरशिलामूर्तिमिव यः ।
स सर्पाणां दर्पं शमयति शकुन्ताधिप इव
ज्वरप्लुष्टान् दृष्ट्या सुखयति सुधाधारसिरया ॥२०॥

Trans. : He who meditates on you in the form of a moon-stone statue, exuding nectar from the myriad rays emanating from your limbs, destroys the arrogance of serpents, like the King of birds, Garuda and cures the fever-ridden with a glance, shedding as it were panaceal nectar.

21

Taṭillēkhātanvīṁ tapanaśaśivaiśvānaramayīṁ
Niṣaṇṇāṁ ṣaṇṇām apyupari kamalānāṁ tava kalām |
Mahāpadmāṭavyāṁ mṛditamalamāyena manasā
Mahāntaḥ paśyanto dadhati paramāhlādalaharīm ||21||

तटिल्लेखातन्वीं तपनशशिवैश्वानरमयीं
निषण्णां षण्णामप्युपरि कमलानां तव कलाम् ।
महापद्माटव्यां मृदितमलमायेन मनसा
महान्तः पश्यन्तो दधति परमाह्लादलहरीम् ॥ २१ ॥

Trans. : Great ones experience the supreme wave of bliss, viewing in their minds cleansed of dirt and ignorance the facet of your form, resplendent like lightning, existing in the sun, moon, and fire as also in the six psychic centres, but above all shining in the thousand-petalled lotus.

22

Bhavāni tvāṁ dāse mayi vitara dṛṣṭiṁ sakaruṇām
Iti stotuṁ vāñchan kathayati bhavāni tvam iti yaḥ |
Tadaiva tvaṁ tasmai diśasi nijasāyujyapadavīṁ
Mukundabrahmendrasphuṭamakuṭanīrājitapadām ||22||

भवानि त्वं दासे मयि वितर दृष्टिं सकरुणा-
मिति स्तोतुं वाञ्छन् कथयति भवानि त्वमिति यः ।
तदैव त्वं तस्मै दिशसि निजसायुज्यपदवीं
मुकुन्दब्रह्मेन्द्रस्फुटमकुटनीराजितपदाम् ॥ २२ ॥

Trans. : Oh ! Creatrix, You bestow the status of the really liberated one, at whose feet the crowns of Viṣṇu, Brahmā, and Indra render homage, on him who says : Oh ! Creatrix, wishing to say : "Oh ! Creatrix, Bestow on this servant of yours your kind glance".

23

Tvayā hṛtvā vāmaṁ vapur aparitṛptena manasā
Śarīrārdhaṁ śaṁbhor aparam api śaṅke hṛtam abhūt |
Yadetat tvadrūpaṁ sakalam aruṇābhaṁ trinayanaṁ
Kucābhyām ānamraṁ kuṭilaśaśicūḍālamakuṭam ||23||

त्वया हृत्वा वामं वपुरपरितृप्तेन मनसा
शरीरार्धं शंभोरपरमपि शङ्के हृतमभूत् ।
यदेतत्त्वद्रूपं सकलमरुणाभं त्रिनयनं
कुचाभ्यामानम्रं कुटिलशशिचूडालमकुटम् ॥ २३ ॥

Trans. : Your form, bent by the weight of the breasts is all-crimson, three-eyed and crescent-crested ; this, I feel, is due to your taking over the other half, being dissatisfied with the left half of the body of the Creator of bliss, already stolen by you.

Notes : This verse highlights the oneness of Śiva and Śakti.

24

Jagatsūte dhātā harir avatī rudraḥ kṣapayate
Tiraskurvannetat svam api vapur īśas tirayati |
Sadāpūrvaḥ sarvaṁ tatidam anugṛhṇāti ca śivas
Tavājñām ālambya kṣaṇacalitayor bhrūlatikayoḥ ||24||

जगत्सूते धाता हरिरवति रुद्रः क्षपयते
तिरस्कुर्वन्नेतत्स्वमपि वपुरीशस्तिरयति ।
सदापूर्वः सर्वं तदिदमनुगृह्णाति च शिव-
स्तवाज्ञामालम्ब्य क्षणचलितयोर्भ्रूलतिकयोः ॥ २४ ॥

Trans. : In deference to the command of your eye-brows moved for a moment, the Creator creates the universe, the Protector protects, the Destroyer destroys ; the Lord, withdrawing all into himself, dissolves his form. The Supremely Auspicious One blesses it all.

Notes : This and the next two verses highlight the subordinance of all gods to the Supreme Power.

25

Trayāṇāṁ devānāṁ triguṇajanitānāṁ tava śive
Bhavet pūjā pūjā tava caraṇayor yā viracitā |
Tathāhi tvadpādodvahanamaṇipīṭhasya nikaṭe
Sthitā hyete śaśvanmukulitakarottaṁsamakuṭāḥ ||25||

त्रयाणां देवानां त्रिगुणजनितानां तव शिवे
भवेत्पूजा पूजा तव चरणयोर्या विरचिता ।
तथाहि त्वत्पादोद्वहनमणिपीठस्य निकटे
स्थिता ह्येते शश्वन्मुकुलितकरोत्तंसमकुटाः ॥ २५ ॥

Trans. : Oh ! Auspicious One, worship rendered to your feet becomes also the worship to the three gods born of the three qualities, for these ever remain near your foot-pedestal with bent crowns and folded hands.

26

Viriñciḥ pañcatvaṁ vrajati harir āpnoti viratiṁ
Vināśaṁ kīnāśo bhajati dhanado yāti nidhanam |
Vitandrī māhendrī vitatir api saṁmīlitadṛśā
Mahāsaṁhāre'smin viharati sati tvatpatir asau ||26||

विरिञ्चिः पञ्चत्वं व्रजति हरिराप्नोति विरतिं
विनाशं कीनाशो भजति धनदो याति निधनम् ।
वितन्द्री माहेन्द्री विततिरपि संमीलितदृशा
महासंहारेऽस्मिन् विहरति सति त्वत्पतिरसौ ॥ २६ ॥

Trans. : Oh ! Supremely Chaste One, the creator dies, the protector dies, the angel of death dies, the lord of wealth dies, the ever-wakeful cluster of gods close their eyes, in this great deluge, only your husband sports with you.

27

Japo jalpaḥ śilpaṁ sakalam api mudrāviracanā
Gatiḥ prādakṣiṇyakramaṇam aśanādyāhutividhiḥ |
Praṇāmaḥ saṁveśaḥ sukham akhilam ātmārpaṇadṛśā
Saparyāparyāyas tava bhavatu yanme vilasitam ||27||

जपो जल्पः शिल्पं सकलमपि मुद्राविरचना
गतिः प्रादक्षिण्यक्रमणमशनाद्याहुतिविधिः ।
प्रणामः संवेशः सुखमखिलमात्मार्पणदृशा
सपर्यापर्यायस्तव भवतु यन्मे विलसितम् ॥ २७ ॥

Trans. : Through the sight of self-surrender, let my prattle become recitation of your name, the movement of my limbs gestures of worship, my walk perambulation around you, my food sacrificial offering, to you, my lying down prostration to you ; whatever I do for my pleasure, let it become transformed into an act of worship to you.

28

Sudhām apyāsvādya pratibhayajarāmṛtyuhariṇīṁ
Vipadyante viśve vidhiśatamakhādyā diviṣadaḥ |
Karālaṁ yatkṣvelaṁ kabalitavataḥ kālakalanā
Na śambhostanmūlaṁ tava janani tāṭaṅkamahimā ||28||

सुधामप्यास्वाद्य प्रतिभयजरामृत्युहरिणीं
विपद्यन्ते विश्वे विधिशतमखाद्या दिविषदः ।
करालं यत्क्ष्वेलं कबलितवतः कालकलना
न शंभोस्तन्मूलं तव जननि ताटङ्कमहिमा ॥ २८ ॥

Trans. : Oh ! Mother, All gods like Brahmā, Indra and others perish even after taking nectar which destroys death, old age, and fear of enemies. But there is no end to the Creator of bliss, who swallowed the most virulent poison. Reason ?—the power of your ear ornaments !

Notes : In India, the belief is that the life-span of the husband is dependent on the chastity of the wife. Married women wear gold ornaments on their ears as a symbol of their wedded bliss, which are removed when the husbands die. In the case of the supreme Mother, the ear ornaments will continue to be worn for ever and Her Lord has as endless a life as her chastity.

29

Kirīṭaṁ vairiñcaṁ parihara puraḥ kaiṭabhabhidaḥ
Kaṭhore koṭīre skhalasi jahi jambhārimakuṭaṁ |
Praṇamreṣveteṣu prasabham upayātasya bhavanaṁ
Bhavasyābhyutthāne tava parijanoktir vijayate ||29||

किरीटं वैरिञ्चं परिहर पुरः कैटभभिदः
कठोरे कोटीरे स्खलसि जहि जम्भारिमकुटम् ।
प्रणम्रेष्वेतेषु प्रसभमुपयातस्य भवनं
भवस्याभ्युत्थाने तव परिजनोक्तिर्विजयते ॥ २९ ॥

Trans. : When you rise and welcome the Creator of bliss arriving home unexpectedly and Brahmā, Viṣṇu, and Indra are prostrating before you, the words of your attendants resound : "Avoid the crown of Viriñci*, don't stumble on the hard crown of Viṣṇu, steer clear of the crown of Indra."

Notes : *Synonym for Brahmā.

30

Svadehodbhūtābhir ghṛṇibhir aṇimādyābhir abhito
Niṣevye nitye tvām aham iti sadā bhāvayati yaḥ |
Kimāścaryaṁ tasya trinayanasamṛddhiṁ tṛṇayato
Mahāsaṁvartāgnir viracayati nīrājanavidhim ||30||

स्वदेहोद्भूताभिर्घृणिभिरणिमाद्याभिरभितो
निषेव्ये नित्ये त्वामहमिति सदा भावयति यः ।
किमाश्चर्यं तस्य त्रिनयनसमृद्धिं तृणयतो
महासंवर्ताग्निर्विरचयति नीराजनविधिम् ॥ ३० ॥

Trans. : Oh ! Immanent One, what is surprising in the fact that the flames of the great Dissolution become a ritual of offering to the one who ever feels : "I worship you surrounded on all sides by the rays of power like *Aṇimā* etc., emanating from your resplendent form" and to whom the prosperity of the Three-eyed One is trifling like grass.

31

Catuḥṣaṣṭyā tantraiḥ sakalam atisandhāya bhuvanaṁ
Sthitas tattatsiddhiprasavaparatantraiḥ paśupatiḥ |
Punas tvannirbandhād akhilapuruṣārthaikaghaṭanā-
Svatantraṁ te tantraṁ kṣititalam avātītarad idam ||31||

चतुःषष्ट्या तन्त्रैः सकलमतिसन्धाय भुवनं
स्थितस्तत्तत्सिद्धिप्रसवपरतन्त्रैः पशुपतिः ।
पुनस्त्वन्निर्बन्धादखिलपुरुषार्थैकघटना-
स्वतन्त्रं ते तन्त्रं क्षितितलमवातीतरदिदम् ॥ ३१ ॥

Trans. : The Lord of creatures, having created the entire universe with the sixty-four *Tantras*, the chief sources of occult powers remained satisfied. But on your insistence, He introduced into the earth this *Tantra* of yours, which bestows all the four aspirations of men : *Dharma*, *Artha*, *Kāma*, and *Mokṣa*.

32

Śivaḥ śaktiḥ kāmaḥ kṣitir atha raviḥ śītakiraṇaḥ
Smaro haṁsaḥ śakras tadanu ca parāmāraharayaḥ |
Amī hṛllekhābhis tisṛbhir avasāneṣu ghaṭitā
Bhajante varṇās te tava janani nāmāvayavatām ||32||

शिवः शक्तिः कामः क्षितिरथ रविः शीतकिरणः
स्मरो हंसः शक्रस्तदनु च परामारहरयः ।
अमी हृल्लेखाभिस्तिसृभिरवसानेषु घटिता
भजन्ते वर्णास्ते तव जननि नामावयवताम् ॥ ३२ ॥

Trans. : Oh ! Mother, The letters : Ka, a, e, la, ha, sa, ka, ha, la, sa, ka, La joined to the three *HRIMS*, become your name and form.

Notes : This stanza gives the secret sixteen-lettered Mantra of *Śrī-Vidyā.*

33

Smaraṁ yoniṁ lakṣmīṁ tritayam idam ādau tava manor
Nidhāyaike nitye niravadhimahābhogarasikāḥ |
Bhajanti tvāṁ cintāmaṇiguṇanibaddhākṣavalayāḥ
Śivāgnau juhvantaḥ surabhighṛtadhārāhutiśataiḥ ||33||

स्मरं योनिं लक्ष्मीं त्रितयमिदमादौ तव मनो-
र्निधायैके नित्ये निरवधिमहाभोगरसिकाः ।
भजन्ति त्वां चिन्तामणिगुणनिबद्धाक्षवलयाः
शिवाग्नौ जुह्वन्तः सुरभिघृतधाराहुतिशतैः ॥ ३३ ॥

Trans. : Oh ! Permanent One, Certain Blessed Ones, desirous of enjoying endless bliss,worship you holding the rosary stringed with stones of the quality of *Cintāmaṇi*, offering oblations made of pure ghee, and reciting the Great *Pañcadaśī* Mantra, prefixing it with the three root-sounds : *KLIM*, *HRIM*, and *SRIM !*

34

Śarīraṁ tvaṁ śaṁbhoḥ śaśimihiravakṣoruhayugaṁ
Tavātmānaṁ manye bhagavati navātmānam anagham |
Ataḥ śeṣaḥ śeṣītyayam ubhayasādhāraṇatayā
Sthitaḥ saṁbandho vāṁ samarasaparānandaparayoḥ ||34||

शरीरं त्वं शंभोः शशिमिहिरवक्षोरुहयुगं
तवात्मानं मन्ये भगवति नवात्मानमनघम् ।
अतः शेषः शेषीत्ययमुभयसाधारणतया
स्थितः संबन्धो वां समरसपरानन्दपरयोः ॥ ३४ ॥

Trans. : Oh ! Resplendent One, You are the body of the Creator of Bliss, with the sun and the moon as your breasts. I consider the Nine-faceted, Pure One as your Self. Thus it is that the epithet : Eternal One is by common usage applicable to you both, Equally, Supremely Blissful Ones.

35

Manas tvaṁ vyoma tvaṁ marud asi marutsārathir asi
Tvam āpas tvaṁ bhūmis tvayi pariṇatāyāṁ na hi param |
Tvam eva svātmānaṁ pariṇamayituṁ viśvavapuṣā
Cidānandākāraṁ śivayuvati bhāvena bibhṛṣe ||35||

मनस्त्वं व्योम त्वं मरुदसि मरुत्सारथिरसि
त्वमापस्त्वं भूमिस्त्वयि परिणतायां न हि परम् ।
त्वमेव स्वात्मानं परिणमयितुं विश्ववपुषा
चिदानन्दाकारं शिवयुवति भावेन बिभृषे ॥ ३५ ॥

Trans. : You are the Mind, you are the Ether, you are Air, you are also Fire and Water, and the Earth. You manifest yourself as the universe, there exists nothing other than you. To transform yourself, who are Consciousness-Bliss into the Universal Body, you deem yourself the young bride of the Auspicious One.

36

Tavājñācakrasthaṁ tapanaśaśikoṭidyutidharaṁ
Paraṁ śaṁbhuṁ vande parimilitapārśvaṁ paracitā |
Yamārādhyan bhaktyā raviśaśiśucīnām aviṣaye
Nirāloke'loke nivasati hi bhālokabhuvane ||36||

तवाज्ञाचक्रस्थं तपनशशिकोटिद्युतिधरं
परं शंभुं वन्दे परिमिलितपार्श्वं परचिता ।
यमाराध्यन् भक्त्या रविशशिशुचीनामविषये
निरालोकेऽलोके निवसति हि भालोकभुवने ॥ ३६ ॥

Trans. : I venerate the Supreme Creator of bliss situated in your *Ājña-Cakra*—between the eye-brows—, resplendent like millions of suns and moons, adorned on his side by the Supreme Power, meditating on whom with devotion, one lives in the effulgent world which needs no light and is beyond the reach of the sun, moon and fire.

Notes : In the six verses commencing from the 36th and ending in the 41st, the Supreme Power is worshipped in the six psychic centres : Ājña, Viśuddhi, Anāhata, Svādhiṣṭhāna, Maṇipūra, and Mūlādhāra.

37

Viśuddhau te śuddhasphaṭikaviśadaṁ vyomajanakaṁ
Śivaṁ seve devīm api śivasamānavyavasitām |
Yayoḥ kāntyā yāntyāḥ śaśikiraṇasārūpyasaraṇer
Vidhūtāntardhvāntā vilasati cakorīva jagatī ||37||

विशुद्धौ ते शुद्धस्फटिकविशदं व्योमजनकं
शिवं सेवे देवीमपि शिवसमानव्यवसिताम् ।
ययोः कान्त्या यान्त्याः शशिकिरणसारूप्यसरणे-
विंधूतान्तर्ध्वान्ता विलसति चकोरीव जगती ॥ ३७ ॥

Trans. : I worship the Auspicious One residing in your *Viśuddhi-Cakra*, shining like a pure crystal, the Creator of ether and you the Goddess of identical disposition ; by the radiance—resembling moonlight—emanating from them, the world enveloped in the darkness of ignorance rejoices, like the *Cakorī*-bird bathing in the rays of the moon.

38

Samunmīlatsaṁvitkamalamakarandaikarasikaṁ
Bhaje haṁsadvandvṁ kim api mahatāṁ mānasacaram |
Yadālāpād aṣṭadaśaguṇitavidyāpariṇatir
Yadādatte doṣād guṇamakhilamadbhyaḥ paya iva ||38||

समुन्मीलत्संवित्कमलमकरन्दैकरसिकं
भजे हंसद्वन्द्वं किमपि महतां मानसचरम् ।
यदालापादष्टादशगुणितविद्यापरिणति-
र्यदादत्ते दोषाद्गुणमखिलमद्भ्यः पय इव ॥ ३८ ॥

Trans. : I worship the two unique swans—*Ham* and *Saḥ*—floating in the minds of the great, who ever enjoy the honey in the full-blown lotus of knowledge and from whose prattle shine the eighteen arts and who sift the good from the evil, like milk from water.

Notes : Swans are supposed to possess the capacity of sifting milk from water.

39

Tava svādhiṣṭhāne hutavahamadhiṣṭhāya niratam
Tam īḍe samvartaṁ janani mahatīṁ tāṁ ca samayām |
Yadāloke lokān dahati mahati krodhakalite
Dayārdrā yā dṛṣṭiḥ śiśiram upacāraṁ racayati ||39||

तव स्वाधिष्ठाने हुतवहमधिष्ठाय निरतं
तमीडे संवर्तं जननि महतीं तां च समयाम् ।
यदालोके लोकान्दहति महति क्रोधकलिते
दयार्द्रा या दृष्टिः शिशिरमुपचारं रचयति ॥ ३९ ॥

Trans. : Oh ! Mother, I bow to the Destroyer who ever remains in your *Svādhiṣṭhāna-Cakra* adopting the form of fire as also to the Great Power, whose glance, tender-wet with kindness, protects by cool healing when the angry look of the Destroyer burns the worlds in the great dissolution.

40

Taṭittvantaṁ śaktyā timiraparipanthisphuraṇayā
Sphurannānāratnābharaṇapariṇaddhendradhanuṣam |
Tava śyāmaṁ meghaṁ kam api maṇipūraikaśaraṇaṁ
Niṣeve varṣantaṁ haramihirataptaṁ tribhuvanam ||40||

तटित्त्वन्तं शक्त्या तिमिरपरिपन्थिस्फुरणया
स्फुरन्नानारत्नाभरणपरिणद्धेन्द्रधनुषम् ।
तव श्यामं मेघं कमपि मणिपूरैकशरणं
निषेवे वर्षन्तं हरमिहिरतप्तं त्रिभुवनम् ॥ ४० ॥

Trans. : I worship the blue, cloud-hued One who has sought refuge in your *Maṇipūra-Cakra* and adorned by lightning through the effulgence of the darkness-destroying Power, shines with the bow of the Indra, studded with various lustrous gems and rains mercy on the three worlds burnt by the destroyer in the great dissolution.

41

Tavādhāre mūle saha samayayā lāsyaparayā
Navātmānaṁ manye navarasamahātāṇḍavanaṭam |
Ubhābhyām etābhyām udayavidhim uddhiśya dayayā
Sanāthābhyāṁ jajñe janakajananīmajjagad idam ||41||

तवाधारे मूले सह समयया लास्यपरया
नवात्मानं मन्ये नवरसमहाताण्डवनटम् ।
उभाभ्यामेताभ्यामुदयविधिमुद्दिश्य दयया
सनाथाभ्यां जज्ञे जनकजननीमज्जगदिदम् ॥ ४१ ॥

Trans. : I meditate on the Nine-faceted One, dancing the great cosmic dance with the nine moods along with the dance-loving Power in your *Mūlādhāra*. This universe becomes reborn mercifully and possessed of a father and mother thanks to these two inseparable Ones.

42

Gatairmāṇikyatvaṁ gaganamaṇibhiḥ sāndraghaṭitaṁ
Kirīṭaṁ te haimaṁ himagirisute kīrtayati yaḥ |
Sa nīḍeyacchāyācchuraṇaśabalaṁ candraśakalaṁ
Dhanuḥ śaunāsīraṁ kim iti na nibadhnāti dhiṣaṇām ||42||

गतैर्माणिक्यत्वं गगनमणिभिः सान्द्रघटितं
किरीटं ते हैमं हिमगिरिसुते कीर्तयति यः ।
स नीडेयच्छायाच्छुरणशबलं चन्द्रशकलं
धनुः शौनासीरं किमिति न निबध्नाति धिषणाम् ॥४२॥

Trans. : Oh ! Daughter of the snowy mountains, he who describes your golden crown studded with gem-like suns would mistake the crescent moon rendered many-splendoured by the lustre of precious stones in the golden crown, as the bow of Indra.

Notes : In the fifty verses commencing from the 42nd, the poet describes the physical form of the Supreme Power from crown to feet.

43

Dhunotu dhvāntaṁ nas tulitadalitendīvaravanaṁ
Ghanasnigdhaślakṣṇaṁ cikuranikurumbaṁ tava śive |
Yadīyaṁ saurabhyaṁ sahajam upalabdhuṁ sumanaso
Vasantyasmin manye balamathanavāṭīviṭapinām ||43||

धुनोतु ध्वान्तं नस्तुलितदलितेन्दीवरवनं
घनस्निग्धश्लक्ष्णं चिकुरनिकुरुम्बं तव शिवे ।
यदीयं सौरभ्यं सहजमुपलब्धुं सुमनसो
वसन्त्यस्मिन्मन्ये बलमथनवाटीविटपिनाम् ॥ ४३ ॥

Trans. : Oh ! Auspicious One, Let the cluster of your hair soft, and dense as the group of full-blown blue lotuses dispel our mental darkness ; the flowers of trees in Indra's garden have come to reside therein with a view to attaining its inherent fragrance, I think.

44

Tanotu kṣemaṁ nas tava vadanasaundaryalaharī-
Parīvāhasrotaḥsaraṇir iva sīmantasaraṇiḥ
Vahantī sindūraṁ prabalakabarībhāratimira-
Dviṣāṁ vṛndair bandīkṛtam iva navīnārkakiraṇam ||44||

तनोतु क्षेमं नस्तव वदनसौन्दर्यलहरी-
परीवाहस्रोतःसरणिरिव सीमन्तसरणिः ।
वहन्ती सिन्दूरं प्रबलकबरीभारतिमिर-
द्विषां वृन्दैर्बन्दीकृतमिव नवीनार्ककिरणम् ॥ ४४ ॥

Trans. : Let the partition of your hair, bearing the *Sindūra*, which resembles the ray of the rising sun imprisoned by the cluster of dense, dark, enemical hair, enhance our welfare ; it looks as if it is the outlet for the flow of the wave of your facial beauty.

45

Arālaiḥ svābhāvyad alikalabhasaśrībhir alakaiḥ
parītaṁ te vaktraṁ parihasati paṅkeruharucim |
Darasmere yasmin daśanarucikiñjalkarucire
Sugandhau mādyanti smaradahanacakṣur madhulihaḥ ||45||

अरालैः स्वाभाव्यादलिकलभसश्रीभिरलकैः
परीतं ते वक्त्रं परिहसति पङ्केरुहरुचिम् ।
दरस्मेरे यस्मिन् दशनरुचिकिञ्जल्करुचिरे
सुगन्धौ माद्यन्ति स्मरदहनचक्षुर्मधुलिहः ॥ ४५ ॥

Trans. : Your face puts to shame the radiance of the lotus, with its gentle smile, rows of beautiful teeth and fragrance ; in it the bee-like eyes of the Destroyer of Cupid drink the honey of bliss ; small curls of frontal hair spread themselves on it like little bees.

46

Lalāṭaṁ lāvaṇyadyutivimalam ābhāti tava yat
Dvidīyaṁ tanmanye makuṭaghaṭitaṁ candraśakalam |
Viparyāsanyāsād ubhayam api saṁbhūya ca mithaḥ
Sudhālepasyūtiḥ pariṇamati rākāhimakaraḥ ||46||

ललाटं लावण्यद्युतिविमलमाभाति तव यत्
द्वितीयं तन्मन्ये मकुटघटितं चन्द्रशकलम् ।
विपर्यासन्यासादुभयमपि संभूय च मिथः
सुधालेपस्यूतिः परिणमति राकाहिमकरः ॥ ४६ ॥

Trans. : I consider your charming, radiant and pure forehead as the second crescent moon attached to your crown ; placed face to face, the two together would turn into the ambrosial full moon.

47

Bhruvau bhugne kiṁcid bhuvanabhayabhaṅgavyasanini
Tvadīye netrābhyāṁ madhukararucibhyāṁ dhṛtaguṇam |
Dhanur manye savyetarakaragṛhītaṁ ratipateḥ
Prakoṣṭhe muṣṭau ca sthagayati nigūḍhāntaram ume ||47||

भ्रुवौ भुग्ने किंचिद्भुवनभयभङ्गव्यसनिनि
त्वदीये नेत्राभ्यां मधुकररुचिभ्यां धृतगुणम् ।
धनुर्मन्ये सव्येतरकरगृहीतं रतिपतेः
प्रकोष्ठे मुष्टौ च स्थगयति निगूढान्तरमुमे ॥ ४७ ॥

Trans. : Oh ! Uma, anxious to dispel the fear of the universe, I deem your slightly bent brows linked to the bee-like eyes to be the bow of Cupid held in his left hand and thus hidden in the middle by the forearm and the fingers.

48

Ahaḥ sūte savyaṁ tava nayanam arkātmakatayā
Triyāmāṁ vāmaṁ te sṛjati rajanīnāyakatayā |
Tṛtīyā te dṛṣṭir daradalitahemāmbujaruciḥ
Samādhatte sandhyāṁ divasaniśayor antaracarīm ||48||

अहः सूते सव्यं तव नयनमर्कात्मकतया
त्रियामां वामं ते सृजति रजनीनायकतया ।
तृतीया ते दृष्टिर्दरदलितहेमाम्बुजरुचिः
समाधत्ते सन्ध्यां दिवसनिशयोरन्तरचरीम् ॥ ४८ ॥

Trans. : Your right eye, being the embodiment of the sun creates day, your left eye being the embodiment of the moon creates night, Your third eye, radiant like the slightly open golden lotus creates twilight, the midpoint between night and day.

49

Viśālā kalyāṇī sphuṭarucir ayodhyā kuvalayaiḥ
Kṛpādhārādhārā kim api madhurābhogavatikā /
Avantī dṛṣṭis te bahunagaravistāravijayā
Dhruvaṁ tattannāmavyavaharaṇayogyā vijayate //49//

विशाला कल्याणी स्फुटरुचिरयोध्या कुवलयैः
कृपाधाराधारा किमपि मधुराभोगवतिका ।
अवन्ती दृष्टिस्ते बहुनगरविस्तारविजया
ध्रुवं तत्तन्नामव्यवहरणयोग्या विजयते ॥ ४९ ॥

Trans. : Your glance is wide, auspicious, impossible for blue lotuses to rival, the base for the flow of kindness, extremely sweet, protective and flourishes like the various capitals, whose names are implied in the words used.

Notes : There is a play on words in this stanza : Viśālā, Kalyāṇī, Ayodhyā, Dhārā, Madhurā, Bhogavatī, Avantī, Vijayā are the names of famous capital towns of ancient India as also words' meanings : wide, auspicious, impossible to rival, flow, sweet, protective, and victorious.

50

Kavīnāṁ sandarbhastabakamakarandaikarasikaṁ
Kaṭākṣavyākṣepabhramarakalabhau karṇayugalam /
Amuñcantau dṛṣṭvā tava navarasāsvādataralā-
Vasūyāsaṁsargād alikanayanaṁ kiṁcid aruṇam //50//

कवीनां सन्दर्भस्तबकमकरन्दैकरसिकं
कटाक्षव्याक्षेपभ्रमरकलभौ कर्णयुगलम् ।
अमुञ्चन्तौ दृष्ट्वा तव नवरसास्वादतरला-
वसूयासंसर्गादलिकनयनं किंचिदरुणम् ॥ ५० ॥

Trans. : Your frontal eye becomes slightly red due to envy, seeing the pair of bee-like eyes intent on tasting the nine emotions and inseparable from the two ears anxious to enjoy the honey of the bunch of flowers which are poets' works.

51

Śive śṛṅgarārdrā taditarajane kutsanaparā
Saroṣā gaṅgāyāṁ giriśacarite vismayavatī |
Harāhibhyo bhītā sarasiruhasaubhāgyajananī
Sakhīṣu smerā te mayi janani dṛṣṭiḥ sakaruṇā ||51||

शिवे शृङ्गारार्द्रा तदितरजने कुत्सनपरा
सरोषा गङ्गायां गिरिशचरिते विस्मयवती ।
हराहिभ्यो भीता सरसिरुहसौभाग्यजननी
सखीषु स्मेरा ते मयि जननि दृष्टिः सकरुणा ॥५१॥

Trans. : Oh ! Mother, Your glance is tender with love towards the Auspicious One, full of aversion to others, angry towards Gaṅgā, full of wonder at the third eye of the Lord, fearful of His snake-ornaments, valiant as the creator of crimson colour in the lotus, smiling towards companions, and compassionate to me.

52

Gate karṇābhyarṇaṁ garuta iva pakṣmāṇi dadhatī
Purāṁ bhettuś cittapraśamarasavidrāvaṇaphale |
Ime netre gotrādharapatikulottaṁsakalike
Tavākarṇākṛṣṭasmaraśaravilāsaṁ kalayataḥ ||52||

गते कर्णाभ्यर्णं गरुत इव पक्ष्माणि दधती
पुरां भेत्तुश्चित्तप्रशमरसविद्रावणफले ।
इमे नेत्रे गोत्राधरपतिकुलोत्तंसकलिके
तवाकर्णाकृष्टस्मरशरविलासं कलयतः ॥ ५२ ॥

Trans. : Oh ! Power who renders the lineage of the snowy mountain ever fragrant, these two eyes of yours which have gone very near the ears, with feather-like lashes are intended to disturb the peace of mind of the Destroyer of Pura, they thus attain the status of Cupid's arrows, drawn upto the ear.

53

Vibhaktatraivarṇyaṁ vyatikaritalīlāñjanatayā
Vibhāti tvannetratritayam idam īśānadayite |
Punaḥ srasṭuṁ devān druhiṇaharirudrānuparatān
Rajaḥ sattvaṁ bibhrat tama iti guṇānāṁ trayam iva ||53||

विभक्तत्रैवर्ण्यं व्यतिकरितलीलाञ्जनतया
विभाति त्वन्नेत्रत्रितयमिदमीशानदयिते ।
पुनः स्रष्टुं देवान् द्रुहिणहरिरुद्रानुपरतान्
रजः सत्त्वं बिभ्रत्तम इति गुणानां त्रयमिव ॥ ५३ ॥

Trans. : Oh ! Beloved of the Lord, these three eyes of yours become tricoloured—red, white, and black—due to your wearing collyrium for adornment. They look like the triad of the three qualities—*Rajas*, *Sattva*, and *Tamas*—intended to create the deities of creation, protection, and destruction dissolved in you at the time of the Great Dissolution.

Notes : The streak of red, seen in the eyes of the great, the natural white of the eyes, and the black of the collyrium make the eyes tricoloured.

54

Pavitrīkartuṁ naḥ paśupatiparādhīnahṛdaye
Dayāmitrair netrair aruṇadhavalaśyāmarucibhiḥ |
Nadah śoṇo gaṅgā tapanatanayeti dhruvam amuṁ
Trayāṇāṁ tīrthānām upanayasi saṁbhedam anagham ||54||

पवित्रीकर्तुं नः पशुपतिपराधीनहृदये
दयामित्रैर्नेत्रैररुणधवलश्यामरुचिभिः ।
नदः शोणो गङ्गा तपनतनयेति ध्रुवममुं
त्रयाणां तीर्थानामुपनयसि संभेदमनघम् ॥ ५४ ॥

Trans. : Oh ! Goddess who have surrendered your heart to the Lord of creatures, by your eyes filled with friendly compassion and adorned by the three colours of red, white, and black you have certainly created this confluence of three sacred rivers : Śoṇabhadrā, Gaṅgā, and Yamunā, in order to purify us.

55

Nimeṣonmeṣābhyāṁ pralayam udayaṁ yāti jagatī
Tavetyāhuḥ santo dharaṇidhararājanyatanaye |
Ṭvadunmeṣājjātaṁ jagad idam aśeṣaṁ pralayataḥ
Paritrātuṁ śaṅke parihṛtanimeṣās tava dṛaśḥ ||55||

निमेषोन्मेषाभ्यां प्रलयमुदयं याति जगती
तवेत्याहुः सन्तो धरणिधरराजन्यतनये ।
त्वदुन्मेषाज्जातं जगदिदमशेषं प्रलयतः
परित्रातुं शङ्के परिहृतनिमेषास्तव दृशः ॥ ५५ ॥

Trans. : Oh ! Daughter of the King of mountains, the learned have said that by the closing and opening of your eyes the universe is destroyed and created. Hence in order to protect this entire universe born out of the opening of your eyes, your eyes ever remain open, without closing, I feel.

56

Tavāparṇe karṇejapanayanapaiśunyacakitā
Nilīyante toye niyatamanimeṣāḥ śapharikāḥ |
Iyaṁ ca śrīr baddhacchadapuṭakavāṭaṁ kuvalayaṁ
Jahāti pratyūṣe niśi ca vighaṭayya praviśati ||56||

तवापर्णे कर्णेजपनयनपैशुन्यचकिता
निलीयन्ते तोये नियतमनिमेषाः शफरिकाः ।
इयं च श्रीर्बद्धच्छदपुटकवाटं कुवलयं
जहाति प्रत्यूषे निशि च विघटय्य प्रविशति ॥ ५६ ॥

Trans. : Oh ! Eternal One, the open-eyed female fishes disappear in water, being afraid of the eyes who carry tales to your ears, this is certain. The goddess of prosperity residing in your eyes deserts the closed blue lotus in the morning and re-enters it opening the petals at night.

Notes : Beautiful eyes of women are always compared to fish and the blue lotus. Here poetic fantasy deems the eyes of the Divine Mother to be superior rivals.

57

Dṛśā drāghīyasyā daradalitanīlotpalarucā
Davīyaṁsaṁ dīnaṁ snapaya kṛpayā mām api śive /
Anenāyaṁ dhanyo bhavati na ca te hānir iyatā
Vane vā harmye vā samakaranipāto himakaraḥ //57//

दृशा द्राघीयस्या दरदलितनीलोत्पलरुचा
दवीयांसं दीनं स्नपय कृपया मामपि शिवे ।
अनेनायं धन्यो भवति न च ते हानिरियता
वने वा हर्म्ये वा समकरनिपातो हिमकरः ॥ ५७ ॥

Trans. : Oh ! Auspicious One, Kindly bathe this poor, distant me with your eyes, reaching upto the ears and resembling the slightly open blue lotus. I shall thus be blessed and there is no harm to you either, for the moon spreads its rays on the forest or the palace alike.

58

Arālaṁ te pālīyugalam agarājanyatanaye
Na keṣām ādhatte kusumaśarakodaṇḍakutukam /
Tiraścīno yatra śravaṇapatham ullaṅghya vilasann-
Apāṅgavyāsaṅgo diśati śarasandhānadhiṣaṇām //58//

अरालं ते पालीयुगलमगराजन्यतनये
न केषामाधत्ते कुसुमशरकोदण्डकुतुकम् ।
तिरश्चीनो यत्र श्रवणपथमुल्लङ्घ्य विलस-
न्नपाङ्गव्यासङ्गो दिशति शरसन्धानधिषणाम् ॥ ५८ ॥

Trans. : Oh ! Daughter of the King of Mountains, the curved space between your eyes and ears creates in everyone the illusion of the bow of Cupid, the One with flowers as arrows ; as a result, the backward glance from the corner of your eyes, crossing the path of the ears resembles the shot of an arrow.

59

Sphuradgaṇḍābhogapratiphalitatāṭaṅgayugalaṁ
Catuścakraṁ manye tava mukham idaṁ manmatharatham |
Yam āruhya druhyatyavaniratham arkenducaraṇaṁ
Mahāvīro māraḥ pramathapataye sajjitavate ||59||

स्फुरद्गण्डाभोगप्रतिफलितताटङ्कयुगलं
चतुश्चक्रं मन्ये तव मुखमिदं मन्मथरथम् ।
यमारुह्य द्रुह्यत्यवनिरथमर्केन्दुचरणं
महावीरो मारः प्रमथपतये सज्जितवते ॥ ५९ ॥

Trans. : I consider this face of yours, reflecting on its pure, mirror-like cheeks the images of the round ear-ornaments, to be the four-wheeled chariot of Cupid, riding which the god of love becomes valorous and fights the Lord of Pramathas*, poised for fight, ascending the chariot of earth, with its wheels of the sun and moon.

Notes : *Śiva.

60

Sarasvatyāḥ sūktīr amṛtalaharīkauśalaharīḥ
Pibantyāḥ śarvāṇi śravaṇaculukābhyām aviralam |
Camatkāraślāghācalitaśirasaḥ kuṇḍalagaṇo
Jhaṇatkārais tāraiḥ prativacanam ācaṣṭa iva te ||60||

सरस्वत्याः सूक्तीरमृतलहरीकौशलहरीः
पिबन्त्याः शर्वाणि श्रवणचुलुकाभ्यामविरलम् ।
चमत्कारश्लाघाचलितशिरसः कुण्डलगणो
झणत्कारैस्तारैः प्रतिवचनमाचष्ट इव ते ॥ ६० ॥

Trans. : Oh ! Beloved of the Lord, ever hearing the sweet praises in your honour sung by the Goddess of Learning, which resemble the flow of nectar, you nod your head in wondrous appreciation and your ear-ornaments seem to endorse the applause, by their resounding clang.

61

Asau nāsāvaṁśas tuhinagirivaṁśadhvajapaṭi
Tvadīyo nedīyaḥ phalatu phalam asmākam ucitam |
Vahatyantarmuktāḥ śiśirakaraniśvāsagalitaṁ
Samṛddhyā yat tāsāṁ bahir api ca muktāmaṇidharaḥ ||61||

असौ नासावंशस्तुहिनगिरिवंशध्वजपटि
त्वदीयो नेदीयः फलतु फलमस्माकमुचितम् ।
वहत्यन्तर्मुक्ताः शिशिरकरनिश्वासगलितं
समृद्ध्या यत्तासां बहिरपि च मुक्तामणिधरः ॥ ६१ ॥

Trans. : Oh ! Flag of the lineage of the snowy Mountain, let this nose of yours, which resembles the bamboo-stalk, bestow on us early, deserving results. It—like the bamboo-stalk—bears pearls inside and due to their abundance, also wears them outside ; these being brought out by the breath passing through the left nostril.

62

Prakṛtyā raktāyās tava sudati dantacchadaruceḥ
Pravakṣye sādṛśyaṁ janayatu phalaṁ vidrumalatā |
Na bimbaṁ tadbimbapratiphalanarāgād aruṇitaṁ
Tulām adhyāroḍhuṁ katham iva vilajjeta kalayā ||62||

प्रकृत्या रक्तायास्तव सुदति दन्तच्छदरुचेः
प्रवक्ष्ये सादृश्यं जनयतु फलं विद्रुमलता ।
न बिम्बं तद्बिम्बप्रतिफलनरागादरुणितं
तुलामध्यारोढुं कथमिव विलज्जेत कलया ॥ ६२ ॥

Trans. : Oh ! Goddess with beautiful teeth, I shall mention an object comparable to your naturally red lips : let the coral-creeper produce a fruit. The *Bimba* fruit has derived its crimson colour by the reflection of your lips ; hence won't it be ashamed to stand comparison even with a small part thereof ?

Notes : The standard comparisons for beautiful women's lips are corals and the *Bimba* fruit. But the poet considers the Divine Mother's lips to be incomparable even to these.

63

Smitajyotsnājālaṁ tava vadanacandrasya pibataṁ
Cakorāṇām āsīd atirasatayā cañcujaḍimā |
Atas te śītāṁśor amṛtalaharīm āmlarucayaḥ
Pibanti svacchandaṁ niśiniśi bhṛśaṁ kāñcikadhiyā ||63||

स्मितज्योत्स्नाजालं तव वदनचन्द्रस्य पिबतां
चकोराणामासीदतिरसतया चञ्चुजडिमा ।
अतस्ते शीतांशोरमृतलहरीमाम्लरुचयः
पिबन्ति स्वच्छन्दं निशिनिशि भृशं काञ्जिकधिया ॥६३॥

Trans. : The *Cakora* birds are satiated with the excessive sweetness of your smile, they have drunk—which is the moonlight emanating from the moon of your face. Hence it is that they, desirous of tasting something sour, drink to their utter satisfaction, night after night the nectar-like waves of rays of the moon, which to them taste like sour gruel.

Notes : The poet is exaggerating the superiority of the Mother's smile to the charm of moonlight.

64

Aviśrāntaṁ patyur guṇagaṇakathāmreḍanajapa
Japāpuṣpacchāyā tava janani jihvā jayati sā |
Yadagrāsīnāyāḥ sphaṭikadṛṣadacchacchavimayī
Sarasvatyā mūrtiḥ pariṇamati māṇikyavapuṣā ||64||

अविश्रान्तं पत्युर्गुणगणकथाम्रेडनजपा
जपापुष्पच्छाया तव जननि जिह्वा जयति सा ।
यदग्रासीनायाः स्फटिकदृषदच्छच्छविमयी
सरस्वत्या मूर्तिः परिणमति माणिक्यवपुषा ॥ ६४ ॥

Trans. : Oh ! Mother, Your tongue, red like the hibiscus flower ever recites the auspicious qualities of your husband. Residing on its tip, the crystal white form of the goddess of learning seems to turn into crimson like the ruby.

65

Raṇe jitvā daityān apahṛtaśirastraiḥ kavacibhir
Nivṛttaiś caṇḍāmaśatripuraharanirmālyavimukhaiḥ |
Viśākhendropendraiḥ śaśiviśadakarpūraśakalā
Vilīyante mātas tava vadanatāmbūlakabalāḥ ||65 ||

रणे जित्वा दैत्यानपहृतशिरस्त्रैः कवचिभि-
र्निवृत्तैश्चण्डांशत्रिपुरहरनिर्माल्यविमुखैः ।
विशाखेन्द्रोपेन्द्रैः शशिविशदकर्पूरशकला
विलीयन्ते मातस्तव वदनताम्बूलकबलाः ॥ ६५ ॥

Trans. : Oh ! Mother, after winning over the demons in battle, the warlords, Subrahmaṇya, Indra, and Viṣṇu return from the front, their helmets in hand, but still wearing the shields and unfit to be given a share of the *Nirmālya* of the Auspicious One, the Destroyer of Tripura, are given by you mouthfuls of dessert, containing camphor, white as the moon, which they eat with relish.

66

Vipañcyā gāyantī vividham apadānaṁ paśupates
Tvayārabdhe vaktuṁ calitaśirasā sādhuvacane |
Tadīyair mādhuryair apalapitatantrīkalaravāṁ
Nijāṁ vīṇāṁ vāṇī niculayati colena nibhṛtam ||66||

विपञ्च्या गायन्ती विविधमपदानं पशुपते-
स्त्वयारब्धे वक्तुं चलितशिरसा साधुवचने ।
तदीयैर्माधुर्यैरपलपिततन्त्रीकलरवां
निजां वीणां वाणी निचुलयति चोलेन निभृतम् ॥६६॥

Trans. : When the goddess of sound plays on the lute the varied legends of the Lord of creatures, you start shaking your head and uttering words of applause. The sweetness of your voice so outrivals that of the lute string that the goddess of sound hides her lute with the cover and makes it silent.

67

Karāgreṇa spṛṣṭaṁ tuhinagiriṇā vatsalatayā
Girīśenodastaṁ muhur adharapānākulatayā |
Karagrāhyaṁ śaṁbhor mukhamukuravṛntaṁ girisute
Kathaṁkāraṁ brūmas tava cubukam aupamyarahitam ||67||

कराग्रेण स्पृष्टं तुहिनगिरिणा वत्सलतया
गिरीशेनोदस्तं मुहुरधरपानाकुलतया ।
करग्राह्यं शंभोर्मुखमुकुरवृन्तं गिरिसुते
कथंकारं ब्रूमस्तव चुबुकमौपम्यरहितम् ॥ ६७ ॥

Trans. : Oh ! Daughter of the Mountain, how can we describe your incomparable chin, which resembles the handle of a mirror, touched in affection with the finger-tip by your father, the Snowy Mountain and lifted again and again by your Lord, desirous of drinking your lips.

68

Bhujāśleṣānnityaṁ puradamayituḥ kaṇṭakavatī
Tava grīvā dhatte mukhakamalanālaśriyam iyam |
Svataḥ śvetā kālāgurubahulajambālamalinā
Mṛṇālīlālityaṁ vahati yad adho hāralatikā ||68||

भुजाश्लेषान्नित्यं पुरदमयितुः कण्टकवती
तव ग्रीवा धत्ते मुखकमलनालश्रियमियम् ।
स्वतः श्वेता कालागुरुबहुलजम्बालमलिना
मृणालीलालित्यं वहति यदधो हारलतिका ॥ ६८ ॥

Trans. : This neck of yours, its hairs standing on end, due to the daily embraces by the arms of the Destroyer of Tripura looks like the stem of the lotus which is your face. The necklace of pearls down below, though inherently white, looks dark due to sandal paste containing other perfume ingredients and resembles the stalk of the lotus leaf.

69

Gale rekhās tisro gatigamakagītaikanipuṇe
Vivāhavyānaddhapraguṇaguṇasaṁkhyāpratibhuvaḥ |
Virājante nānāvidhamadhurarāgākarabhuvāṁ
Trayāṇāṁ grāmāṇāṁ sthitiniyamasīmāna iva te ||69||

गले रेखास्तिस्रो गतिगमकगीतैकनिपुणे
विवाहव्यानद्धप्रगुणगुणसंख्याप्रतिभुवः ।
विराजन्ते नानाविधमधुररागाकरभुवां
त्रयाणां ग्रामाणां स्थितिनियमसीमान इव ते ॥ ६९ ॥

Trans. : Oh! Goddess expertly versed in the nuances of music, the three lines on your neck, reminiscent of the three marital chords tied by your Lord at the time of marriage shine like the boundary lines of the three villages which are the source of the various sweet melodies.

Notes : Three lines, seen on the forehead, neck or the stomach are auspicious signs associated with the great.

Ṣaḍja, Madhyama, and Gāndhara are the three villages considered to be the source of the major Indian melodies.

70

Mṛṇālīmṛdvīnāṁ tava bhujalatānāṁ catasṛṇāṁ
Caturbhiḥ saundaryaṁ sarasijabhavaḥ stauti vadanaiḥ /
Nakhebhyaḥ saṁtrasyan prathamamathanād andhakaripoś
Caturṇāṁ śīrṣāṇāṁ samamabhayahastārpaṇadhiyā //70//

मृणालीमृद्वीनां तव भुजलतानां चतसृणां
चतुर्भिः सौन्दर्यं सरसिजभवः स्तौति वदनैः ।
नखेभ्यः संत्रस्यन् प्रथममथनादन्धकरिपो-
श्चतुर्णां शीर्षाणां सममभयहस्तार्पणधिया ॥ ७० ॥

Trans. : The angel of creation born out of the lotus, being afraid of the nails of your Lord, the Enemy of Andhaka who had clipped off one of his heads earlier praises with his remaining four faces the beauty of your four hands, soft like the lotus-creepers, seeking simultaneous protection for his heads.

Notes : The Great God is believed to have punished Brahmā, the Deity of creation by clipping off one of his five heads, for succumbing to a fit of passion.

The Divine Mother is supposed to have four symbolic hands.

71

Nakhānāmudyotair navanalinarāgaṁ vihasatāṁ
Karāṇāṁ te kāntiṁ kathaya kathayāmaḥ katham ume /
Kayācid vā sāmyaṁ bhajatu kalayā hanta kamalaṁ
Yadi krīḍallakṣmīcaraṇatalalākṣārasacaṇam //71//

नखानामुद्योतैर्नवनलिनरागं विहसतां
करार्णां ते कान्तिं कथय कथयामः कथमुमे ।
कयाचिद्वा साम्यं भजतु कलया हन्त कमलं
यदि क्रीडल्लक्ष्मीचरणतललाक्षारसचणम् ॥ ७१ ॥

Trans. : Oh ! Uma, kindly tell us, how do we describe the attractive beauty of your hands which put to shame, with the radiance of the nails, the grace of the newly open red lotus at dawn. It is a pity that even by the association with the red colouring in the feet of the goddess of prosperity which play on it, the red lotus cannot equal even one sixteenth of the beauty of your hands.

72

Samaṁ devi skandadvipavadanapītaṁ stanayugaṁ
Tavedaṁ naḥ khedaṁ haratu satataṁ prasnutamukham |
Yad ālokyāśaṅkākulitahṛdayo hāsajanakaḥ
Svakumbhau herambaḥ parimṛśati hastena jhaḍiti ||72||

समं देवि स्कन्दद्विपवदनपीतं स्तनयुगं
तवेदं नः खेदं हरतु सततं प्रस्नुतमुखम् ।
यदालोक्याशङ्काकुलितहृदयो हासजनकः
स्वकुम्भौ हेरम्बः परिमृशति हस्तेन झडिति ॥ ७२ ॥

Trans. : Oh ! Goddess, let this pair of your breasts, their nipples exuding milk at the sight of your children and simultaneously drunk by Kumāra and Gaṇeśa dispel our sorrow. Seeing them, the Elephant-faced One anxiously and hastily feels his temples with his hand, evoking laughter in you and the Lord.

Notes : The poet is fancifully exploiting the oft-used comparison of beautiful women's breasts to the temples of elephants.

73

Amū te vakṣojāvamṛtarasamāṇikyakutupau
Na saṁdehaspando nagapatipatāke manasi naḥ |
Pibantau tau yasmād aviditavadhūsaṅgarasikau
Kumārāvadyāpi dviradavadanakrauñcadalanau ||73||

अमू ते वक्षोजावमृतरसमाणिक्यकुतुपौ
न संदेहस्पन्दो नगपतिपताके मनसि नः ।
पिबन्तौ तौ यस्माद्विदितवधूसङ्गरसिकौ
कुमारावद्यापि द्विरदवदनक्रौञ्चदलनौ ॥ ७३ ॥

Trans. : Oh ! Goddess who are like the banner of the King of Mountains, There are no doubts in our minds that these breasts of yours are the jewelled chalices of nectar ; for your two sons, the Elephant-faced One and Kārtikeya, the slayer of the demon Krauñca, who have drunk at them, remain even today infants, innocent of sexual desire.

Notes : Passing from childhood to youth and then to old age is the sign of decay and death, which does not occur in the case of the immortal children of the Divine Mother.

74

Vahatyamba stamberamadanujakumbhaprakṛtibhiḥ
Samārabdhāṁ muktāmaṇibhir amalāṁ hāralatikāṁ |
Kucābhogo bimbādhararucibhir antaḥśabalitāṁ
Pratāpavyāmiśrāṁ puradamayituḥ kīrtim iva te ||74||

वहत्यम्ब स्तम्बेरमदनुजकुम्भप्रकृतिभिः
समारब्धां मुक्तामणिभिरमलां हारलतिकाम् ।
कुचाभोगो बिम्बाधररुचिभिरन्तःशबलितां
प्रतापव्यामिश्रां पुरदमयितुः कीर्तिमिव ते ॥ ७४ ॥

Trans. : Oh ! Mother, the middle region of your breasts wears a pearl necklace, made of the most superior pearls taken from the temples of the elephant-faced demon, which is pure white and yet of variegated colour inside, due to the reflection of your lips, red like the *Bimba* fruit—thus resembling the pure reputation of your Lord, the Destroyer of Tripura, mingled with His valour and prowess.

75

Tava stanyaṁ manye dharaṇidharakanye hṛdayataḥ
Payaḥpārāvāraḥ parivahati sārasvatam iva |
Dayāvatyā dattaṁ draviḍaśiśur āsvādya tava yat
Kavīnāṁ prauḍhānām ajani kamanīyaḥ kavayitā ||75||

तव स्तन्यं मन्ये धरणिधरकन्ये हृदयतः
पयःपारावारः परिवहति सारस्वतमिव ।
दयावत्या दत्तं द्रविडशिशुरास्वाद्य तव यत्
कवीनां प्रौढानामजनि कमनीयः कवयिता ॥ ७५ ॥

Trans. : Oh ! Daughter of the Mountain, I consider the milk flowing from your breasts to be the ocean of nectar originating from your heart and that it flows like a current of learning ; for drinking it so kindly given by you, this child of the Draviḍa region has become an author of works, which attract the minds of reputed poets.

Notes : Śaṅkara, born in Kerala, calls himself the child of the Draviḍa region, drinking at the breasts of the Divine Mother the milk of poesy.

76

Harakrodhajvālāvalibhir avalīḍhena vapuṣā
Gabhīre te nābhīsarasī kṛtasaṅgo manasijaḥ |
Samuttasthau tasmād acalatanaye dhūmalatikā
Janas tāṁ jānīte tava janani romāvalir iti ||76||

हरक्रोधज्वालावलिभिरवलीढेन वपुषा
गभीरे ते नाभीसरसि कृतसङ्गो मनसिजः ।
समुत्तस्थौ तस्मादचलतनये धूमलतिका
जनस्तां जानीते तव जननि रोमावलिरिति ॥ ७६ ॥

Trans. : Oh ! Mother, Oh ! Daughter of the Mountain, when his body was enveloped by the flames of the Destroyer's anger, Cupid plunged into the deep pond which is your navel ; the world considers the resultant line of smoke which arose to be the hair line rising from your navel.

77

Yadetat kālindītanutarataraṅgākṛti śive
Kṛśe madhye kiṁcijjanani tava yad bhāti sudhiyām |
Vimardād anyonyaṁ kucakalaśayor antaragataṁ
Tanūbhūtaṁ vyoma praviśad iva nābhiṁ kuhariṇīm ||77||

यदेतत्कालिन्दीतनुतरतरङ्गाकृति शिवे
कृशे मध्ये किंचिज्जननि तव यद्भाति सुधियाम् ।
विमर्दादन्योन्यं कुचकलशयोरन्तरगतं
तनूभूतं व्योम प्रविशदिव नाभिं कुहरिणीम् ॥ ७७ ॥

Trans. : Oh ! Auspicious One, Oh ! Mother, this thin line of hair above your slender waist, looking like the minute wave of the dark Yamunā river in the eyes of the wise, also gives the impression that the minute space between your potlike breasts seems to enter the deep navel escaping from the mutual pressure exerted by them.

78

Sthiro gaṅgāvartaḥ stanamukularomāvalilatā-
Kalāvālaṁ kuṇḍaṁ kusumaśaratejohutabhujaḥ |
Rater līlāgāraṁ kim api tava nābhir girisute
Biladvāraṁ siddher giriśanayanānāṁ vijayate ||78||

स्थिरो गङ्गावर्तः स्तनमुकुलरोमावलिलता-
कलावालं कुण्डं कुसुमशरतेजोहुतभुजः ।
रतेर्लीलागारं किमपि तव नाभिर्गिरिसुते
बिलद्वारं सिद्धेर्गिरिशनयनानां विजयते ॥ ७८ ॥

Trans. : Oh ! Daughter of the Mountain, your navel flourishes as the still current of river Gaṅgā, as the bed for the hair creeper supporting the lotus-buds of your breasts, as the firepit for the flame of Cupid's magnetism, as the sport resort of Ratī, Cupid's wife, and as the entrance to the cave where the penance of the eyes of your Lord attains its goal.

79

Nisargakṣīṇasya stanataṭabhareṇa klamajuṣo
Namanmūrter nārītilaka śanakais truṭyta iva |
Ciraṁ te madhyasya truṭitataṭinītīrataruṇa
Samāvasthāsthemno bhavatu kuśalaṁ śailatanaye ||79||

निसर्गक्षीणस्य स्तनतटभरेण क्लमजुषो
नमन्मूर्तेर्नारीतिलक शनकैस्त्रुट्यत इव ।
चिरं ते मध्यस्य त्रुटिततटिनीतीरतरुणा
समावस्थास्थेम्नो भवतु कुशलं शैलतनये ॥ ७९ ॥

Trans. : Oh ! Ideal of womanhood, Oh ! Daughter of the Mountain, let your waist, inherently slender and strained by the weight of the breasts, gradually bending as if to break,—thus in a state similar to that of a tree on a river-bank washed away by the floods,—be ever safe !

80

Kucau sadyaḥ svidyattaṭaghaṭitakūrpāsabhidurau
Kaṣantau dormūle kanakakalaśābhau kalayatā |
Tava trātuṁ bhaṅgād alam iti valagnaṁ tanubhuvā
Tridhā naddhaṁ devi trivali lavalīvallibhir iva ||80||

कुचौ सद्यः स्विद्यत्तटघटितकूर्पासभिदुरौ
कषन्तौ दोर्मूले कनककलशाभौ कलयता ।
तव त्रातुं भङ्गादलमिति वलग्नं तनुभुवा
त्रिधा नद्धं देवि त्रिवलि लवलीवल्लिभिरिव ॥ ८० ॥

Trans. : Oh ! Goddess, Your waist appears to be bound by the three folds of your stomach, as if by *Lavalī* creepers, lest it be hurt by the weight of the breasts through the machination of Cupid who created the two golden pot-like breasts, which rub against the sides and try to burst out of their sweaty garment, the moment you think of your Lord.

81

Gurutvaṁ vistāraṁ kṣitidharapatiḥ pārvati nijān-
Nitambād acchidya tvayi haraṇarūpeṇa nidadhe |
Atas te vistīrṇo gurur ayam aśeṣāṁ vasumatīṁ
Nitambaprāgbhāraḥ sthagayati laghutvaṁ nayati ca ||81||

गुरुत्वं विस्तारं क्षितिधरपतिः पार्वति निजा-
न्नितम्बादाच्छिद्य त्वयि हरणरूपेण निदधे ।
अतस्ते विस्तीर्णो गुरुरयमशेषां वसुमतीं
नितम्बप्राग्भारः स्थगयति लघुत्वं नयति च ॥८१॥

Trans. : Oh ! Daughter of the Mountain, the King of mountains, took heaviness and expanse from his flanks and gave them as dowry to you. Hence this hip of yours is heavy and expansive ; it hides the earth and makes it light.

82

Karīndrāṇāṁ śuṇḍān kanakakadalīkāṇḍapaṭalīm
Ubhābhyām ūrubhyām ubhayam api nirjitya bhavati |
Suvṛttābhyāṁ patyuḥ praṇatikaṭhinābhyāṁ girisute
Vidhijñe jānubhyāṁ vibudhakarikumbhadvayam asi ||82 ||

करीन्द्राणां शुण्डान् कनककदलीकाण्डपटली-
उभाभ्यामूरुभ्यामुभयमपि निर्जित्य भवति ।
सुवृत्ताभ्यां पत्युः प्रणतिकठिनाभ्यां गिरिसुते
विधिज्ञे जानुभ्यां विबुधकरिकुम्भद्वयमसि ॥ ८२ ॥

Trans. : Oh ! Daughter of the Mountain, Oh ! Knower of the Art of Love, You remain victorious, defeating with your two thighs the trunks of wild elephants and the golden plantain stalks and with your two beautiful rounded knees hardened by prostration to your Lord the two temples of Indra's elephant.

83

Parājetuṁ rudraṁ dviguṇaśaragarbhau girisute
Niṣaṅgau jaṅghe te viṣamaviśikho bāḍham akṛta |
Yadagre dṛśyante daśaśaraphalāḥ pādayugalī-
Nakhāgracchadmanaḥ suramakuṭaśāṇaikaniśitāḥ ||83||

पराजेतुं रुद्रं द्विगुणशरगर्भौ गिरिसुते
निषङ्गौ जङ्घे ते विषमविशिखो बाढमकृत ।
यदग्रे दृश्यन्ते दशशरफलाः पादयुगली-
नखाग्रच्छद्मानः सुरमकुटशाणैकनिशिताः ॥ ८३ ॥

Trans. : Oh ! Daughter of the Mountain, it is certain that Cupid, who possesses mischievous arrows made two quivers out of your two lower legs to hold twice the number of arrows in order to defeat the Lord, the Destroyer, for at their ends are seen ten edges of arrows, sharpened mainly on the crowns of angels which appear to be the nails of your toes.

Notes : The toe-nails of the Divine Mother are said to be sharpened by the crowns of angels, since they are constantly prostrating at her feet.

84

Śrutīnāṁ mūrdhāno dadhati tava yau śekharatayā
Mamāpyetau mātaḥ śirasi dayayā dhehi caraṇau |
Yayoḥ pādyaṁ pāthaḥ paśupatijaṭājūṭataṭinī
Yayor lākṣālakṣmīraruṇaharicūḍāmaṇiruciḥ ||84||

श्रुतीनां मूर्धानो दधति तव यौ शेखरतया
ममाप्येतौ मातः शिरसि दयया धेहि चरणौ ।
ययोः पाद्यं पाथः पशुपतिजटाजूटतटिनी
ययोर्लाक्षालक्ष्मीररुणहरिचूडामणिरुचिः ॥ ८४ ॥

Trans. : Oh ! Mother, kindly place these feet of yours on my head too. The *Upaniṣads*, which are the crowning glory of the *Vedas* wear them like flowers for adornment ; River Gaṅgā who resides in the matted hair of the Lord of creatures waters them in worship ; the radiance of the red colouring on them is that of the red ruby on the crown of Viṣṇu.

85

Namovākaṁ brūmo nayanaramaṇīyāya padayos
Tavāsmai dvandvāya sphuṭarucirasālaktakavate |
Asūyatyatyantaṁ yadabhihananāya spṛhayate
Paśūnāmīśānaḥ pramadavanakaṅkelitarave ||85||

नमोवाकं ब्रूमो नयनरमणीयाय पदयो-
स्तवास्मै द्वन्द्वाय स्फुटरुचिरसालक्तकवते ।
असूयत्यत्यन्तं यदभिहननाय स्पृहयते
पशूनामीशानः प्रमदवनकङ्केलितरवे ॥ ८५ ॥

Trans. : Let us say : Prostrations to these two feet of yours so pleasing to the eyes and so full of effulgence and coloured red by the wet vegetable dye. The Lord of creatures is jealous of the *Aśoka* trees in the garden which yearn to be trodden by your feet.

Notes : It is a belief that *Aśoka* trees flower only if they are trodden by the feet of young women. The Divine Lover is so possessive that He cannot bear to see the feet of the Goddess come into contact even with the *Aśoka* trees !

86

Mṛṣā kṛtvā gotraskhalanam atha vailakṣyanamitaṁ
Lalāṭe bhartāraṁ caraṇakamale tāḍayati te |
Cirād antaḥśalyaṁ dahanakṛtam unmūlitavatā
Tulākoṭikvāṇaiḥ kilikilitam īśānaripuṇā ||86||

मृषा कृत्वा गोत्रस्खलनमथ वैलक्ष्यनमितं
ललाटे भर्तारं चरणकमले ताडयति ते ।
चिरादन्तःशल्यं दहनकृतमुन्मूलितवता
तुलाकोटिक्वाणैः किलिकिलितमीशानरिपुणा ॥८६॥

Trans. : When your lotus-like feet strike your Lord on the forehead, during love-play, as He pretends to be in love with another and mentions her name and puts His head down in shame, Cupid completely gets rid of his long cherished rancour against the Lord for burning him and proclaims his victory through the jingling of your anklets.

87

Himānīhantavyaṁ himagirinivāsaikacaturau
Niśāyaṁ nidrāṇaṁ niśi caramabhāge ca viśadau |
Varaṁ lakṣmīpātraṁ śriyamatisṛjantau samayināṁ
Sarojaṁ tvatpādau janani jayataś citram iha kim ||87||

हिमानीहन्तव्यं हिमगिरिनिवासैकचतुरौ
निशायां निद्राणं निशि चरमभागे च विशदौ ।
वरं लक्ष्मीपात्रं श्रियमतिसृजन्तौ समयिनां
सरोजं त्वत्पादौ जननि जयतश्चित्रमिह किम् ॥ ८७ ॥

Trans. : Oh ! Mother, it is hardly surprising that your feet outrival the lotus, the blessed residence of the goddess of prosperity. Its petals drop in cold weather and droop at night, while your feet remain open, unaffected by their residence in the snowy mountain and even at night. They bestow endless prosperity on those who worship you along the pure *Samaya* path.

Notes : *Samaya* worship is through the mind, as opposed to external rituals.

88

Padaṁ te kīrtīnāṁ prapadam apadaṁ devi vipadāṁ
Kathaṁ nītaṁ sadbhiḥ kaṭhinakamaṭhīkarparatulām /
Kathaṁ vā bāhubhyām upayamanakāle purabhidā
Yad ādāya nyastaṁ dṛṣadi dayamānena manasā //88//

पदं ते कीर्तीनां प्रपदमपदं देवि विपदां
कथं नीतं सद्भिः कठिनकमठीकर्परतुलाम् ।
कथं वा बाहुभ्यामुपयमनकाले पुरभिदा
यदादाय न्यस्तं दृषदि दयमानेन मनसा ।। ८८ ।।

Trans. : Oh ! Goddess, how have the poets compared to the hard back of the tortoise the top of your feet, which is the source of your reputation in protecting your devotees and is no place for dangers ? How could the Enemy of Tripura, with his heart full of mercy lift it and place it on the grinding stone, at the time of marriage ?

Notes : The back of the tortoise is a standard comparison for the top of shapely feet. Placing the foot of the bride on a grinding stone is a part of the wedding ceremony according to Vedic rites. The poet is ridiculing the heartless treatment meted out to the Mother's tender feet by poets and the Lord.

89

Nakhair nākastrīṇāṁ karakamalasaṁkocaśaśibhis
Tarūṇāṁ divyānāṁ hasata iva te caṇḍi caraṇau /
Phalāni svaḥsthebhyaḥ kisalayakarāgreṇa dadatāṁ
Daridrebhyo bhadrāṁ śriyam aniśam ahnāya dadatau //89//

नखैर्नाकस्त्रीणां करकमलसंकोचशशिभि-
स्तरूणां दिव्यानां हसत इव ते चण्डि चरणौ ।
फलानि स्वःस्थेभ्यः किसलयकराग्रेण ददतां
दरिद्रेभ्यो भद्रां श्रियमनिशमह्नाय ददतौ ॥ ८६ ॥

Trans. : Oh ! Goddess who slew the demon Caṇḍa, Your feet which ever bestow full prosperity on the poor the moment asked for, laugh at the *Kalpaka* trees in heaven which grant fruits, through their tender shoots, only to the celestial angels, and (laugh also) at the celestial women through (your ten) nails which resemble (ten) moons and make them close their lotus-hands.

90

Dadāne dīnebhyaḥ śriyam aniśam āśānusadṛśīm
Amandaṁ saundaryaprakaramakarandaṁ vikirati /
Tavāsmin mandārastabakasubhage yātu caraṇe
Nimajjan majjīvaḥ karaṇacaraṇaḥ ṣaṭcaraṇatām //90//

ददाने दीनेभ्यः श्रियमनिशमाशानुसदृशी-
ममन्दं सौन्दर्यप्रकरमकरन्दं विकिरति ।
तवास्मिन्मन्दारस्तबकसुभगे यातु चरणे
निमज्जन्मज्जीवः करणचरणः षट्चरणताम् ॥ ९० ॥

Trans. : Let my life, with its six sensory organs, attain the status of the six-footed bee, entering this lotus of your feet, which ever gives to the poor riches according to their desire, exudes the honey of boundless beauty and is as pretty as a bunch of *Kalpaka* flowers.

Notes : The six sensory organs are : the mind and the five senses of sight, hearing, taste, touch and smell.

91

Padanyāsakrīḍāparicayam ivārabdhumanasaḥ
Skhalantas te khelaṁ bhavanakalahaṁsā na jahati |
Atas teṣāṃ śikṣāṁ subhagamaṇimañjīraraṇita-
Cchalād ācakṣāṇaṁ charaṇakamalaṁ chārucarite ||91||

पदन्यासक्रीडापरिचयमिवारब्धुमनसः
स्खलन्तस्ते खेलं भवनकलहंसा न जहति ।
अतस्तेषां शिक्षां सुभगमणिमञ्जीररणित-
च्छलादाचक्षाणं चरणकमलं चारुचरिते ॥ ९१ ॥

Trans. : Oh ! Goddess with beautiful gait, the swans of your home, anxious to learn the graceful steps of your feet do not give up imitation of your gait, though tripping up again and again. Hence the lotus of your feet seems to teach them the correct step through the jingling of your anklets, wrought with precious gems.

Notes : Normally the gait of the swan is the ideal to which the gait of beautiful women is compared. Here the poet is making the swans learn the correct gait from the Divine Mother.

92

Gatās te mañcatvaṁ druhiṇaharirudreśvarabhṛtaḥ
Śivaḥ svacchacchāyaghaṭitakapaṭapracchadapaṭḥ |
Tvadīyanaṁ bhāsāṁ pratiphalanarāgāruṇataya
Śarīrī śṛṅgāro rasa iva dṛśāṁ dogdhi kutukam ||92||

गतास्ते मञ्चत्वं द्रुहिणहरिरुद्रेश्वरभृतः
शिवः स्वच्छच्छायाघटितकपटप्रच्छदपटः ।
त्वदीयानां भासां प्रतिफलनरागारुणतया
शरीरी शृङ्गारो रस इव दृशां दोग्धि कुतुकम् ॥ ९२ ॥

Trans. : All the deities of creation, protection and destruction have been absorbed into your bed. The Auspicious One, enveloped as it were by the cover of his white effulgence and appearing crimson by the reflection of the rays emanating from you, looks pleasing to the eyes as if He is the embodiment of the essence of love.

93

Arālā keśeṣu prakṛtisaralā mandahasite
Śirīṣābhā citte dṛṣadupalaśobhā kucataṭe |
Bhṛśaṁ tanvī madhye pṛthur urasijārohaviṣaye
Jagattrātuṁ śambhor jayati karuṇā kācid aruṇā ||93||

अराला केशेषु प्रकृतिसरला मन्दहसिते
शिरीषाभा चित्ते दृषदुपलशोभा कुचतटे ।
भृशं तन्वी मध्ये पृथुरुरसिजारोहविषये
जगत्त्रातुं शंभोर्जयति करुणा काचिदरुणा ॥ ९३ ॥

Trans. : The Gracious Power of the Auspicious One, crimson in colour flourishes to protect the universe, curly in hair, inherently artless in smile, soft as the *Sirīṣa* flower in heart, hard and shining like a diamond in the region of the breasts, very slender in the waist and expansive in hips.

94

Kalaṅkaḥ kastūrī rajanikarabimbaṁ jalamayaṁ
Kalābhiḥ karpūrair marakatakaraṇḍaṁ nibiḍitam |
Atas tvadbhogena pratidinam idaṁ riktakuharaṁ
Vidhir bhūyo bhūyo nibiḍayati nunaṁ tava kṛte ||94||

कलङ्कः कस्तूरी रजनिकरबिम्बं जलमयं
कलाभिः कर्पूरैर्मरकतकरण्डं निबिडितम् ।
अतस्त्वद्भोगेन प्रतिदिनमिदं रिक्तकुहरं
विधिर्भूयो भूयो निबिडयति नूनं तव कृते ॥ ९४ ॥

Trans.: The stain on the moon is musk, the moon is water contained in an emerald tub and mixed with camphor which is moon's rays. Seeing this daily emptied by your enjoyment the creator fills it gradually for your sake, this is certain.

Notes: The poet is visualising that the waning of the moon is due to the Goddess's usage of perfumed water contained in it for her daily bath and the waxing due to the replenishment effected by the creator.

95

Purārāter antaḥpuram asi tatas tvaccharaṇayoḥ
Saparyāmaryādā taralakaraṇānām asulabhā |
Tathā hyete nītāḥ śatamakhamukhāḥ siddhim atulāṁ
Tava dvāropāntasthitibhir aṇimādyābhir amarāḥ ||95||

पुरारातेरन्तःपुरमसि ततस्त्वच्चरणयोः
सपर्यामर्यादा तरलकरणानामसुलभा ।
तथा ह्येते नीताः शतमखमुखाः सिद्धिमतुलां
तव द्वारोपान्तस्थितिभिरणिमाद्याभिरमराः ॥ ९५ ॥

Trans.: You are the consort of the Supreme Lord, the Destroyer of Tripura. Hence the proximate worship of your feet is not possible for the fickle-minded; that is why gods like Indra have been kept satisfied at the gate by your subordinate powers like *Aṇimā*.

96

Kalatraṁ vaidhātraṁ katikati bhajante na kavayaḥ
Śriyo devyāḥ ko vā na bhavati patiḥ kair api dhanaiḥ |
Mahādevaṁ hitvā tava sati satīnam acarame
Kucābhyām āsaṅgaḥ kuravakataror apyasulabhaḥ ||96||

कलत्रं वैधात्रं कतिकति भजन्ते न कवयः
श्रियो देव्याः को वा न भवति पतिः कैरपि धनैः ।
महादेवं हित्वा तव सति सतीनामचरमे
कुचाभ्यामासङ्गः कुरवकतरोरप्यसुलभः ॥ ९६ ॥

Trans. : Oh ! Chaste One, Oh ! Ideal of pure womanhood, many poets attain the goddess of learning, the consort of the creator ; through various types of riches, many become lords of the goddess of prosperity ; but the contact of your breasts is available to none other than the Great God – not even to the *Kuravaka* tree.

97

Girām āhur devīṁ druhiṇagṛhiṇīm āgamavido
Hareḥ patnīṁ padmāṁ harasahacarīm adritanayām |
Turīyā kāpi tvaṁ duradhigamaniḥsīmamahimā
Mahāmāyā viśvaṁ bhramayasi parabrahmamahiṣi ||97||

गिरामाहुर्देवीं द्रुहिणगृहिणीमागमविदो
हरेः पत्नीं पद्मां हरसहचरीमद्रितनयाम् ।
तुरीया कापि त्वं दुरधिगमनिःसीममहिमा
महामाया विश्वं भ्रमयसि परब्रह्ममहिषि ॥ ९७ ॥

Trans. : Oh ! Queen of the Supreme God, the learned ones have deemed you as the goddess of learning, wife of the creator, as the goddess of riches, wife of the protector as the daughter of the Mountain, the partner of the Destroyer. But you as a mysterious, illusory fourth Power with an inaccessible, infinite greatness dazzle the universe.

98

Kadā kāle mātaḥ kathaya kalitālaktakarasaṁ
Pibeyaṁ vidyārthī tava caraṇanirṇejanajalam |
Prakṛtyā mūkānām api ca kavitākāraṇatayā
Kadā dhatte vāṇīmukhakamalatāmbūlarasatām ||98||

कदा काले मातः कथय कलितालक्तकरसं
पिबेयं विद्यार्थी तव चरणनिर्णेजनजलम् ।
प्रकृत्या मूकानामपि च कविताकारणतया
कदा धत्ते वाणीमुखकमलताम्बूलरसताम् ॥ ९८ ॥

Trans. : Oh ! Mother, tell me : when can this disciple drink the water which has washed your feet and thus mixed with the red vegetable dye colouring them, which by making even those who are dumb by birth poets resembles the red dessert juice from the lotus mouth of the goddess of learning.

99

Sarasvatyā lakṣmyā vidhiharisapatno viharate
Rateḥ pātivratyaṁ śithilayati ramyeṇa vapuṣā |
Ciraṁ jīvanneva kṣapitapaśupāśavyatikaraḥ
Parānandābhikhyaṁ rasayati rasaṁ tvadbhajanavan ||99||

सरस्वत्या लक्ष्म्या विधिहरिसपत्नो विहरते
रतेः पातिव्रत्यं शिथिलयति रम्येण वपुषा ।
चिरं जीवन्नेव क्षपितपशुपाशव्यतिकरः
परानन्दाभिख्यं रसयति रसं त्वद्भजनवान् ॥ ९९ ॥

Trans. : Your devotee sports with learning and riches as the rival of the creator and protector, with a dazzling body shatters the fixity of mind of Cupid's wife, and freed from the bondage of birth and ignorance, lives long and enjoys the essence of Supreme Bliss.

100

Pradīpajvālābhir divasakaranīrājanavidhiḥ
Sudhāsūteś candropalajalalavair arghyaracanā |
Svakīyair ambhobhiḥ salilanidhisauhityakaraṇaṁ
Tvadīyābhir vāgbhis tava janani vācāṁ stutir iyam ||100||

प्रदीपज्वालाभिर्दिवसकरनीराजनविधिः
सुधासूतेश्चन्द्रोपलजललवैरर्घ्यरचना ।
स्वकीयैरम्भोभिः सलिलनिधिसौहित्यकरणं
त्वदीयाभिर्वाग्भिस्तव जननि वाचां स्तुतिरियम् ॥१००॥

Trans. : Oh! Mother, This praise of words in your honour composed with your own words is like the worship of lights in honour of the sun done with its own rays, the oblation in honour of the moon with the water emanating from the moon-stone, and the pleasing of the ocean with its own waters.

इति श्रीमत्परमहंसपरिव्राजकाचार्यस्य श्रीगोविन्दभगवत्पूज्यपादशिष्यस्य
श्रीमच्-शङ्कर-भगवतः कृतिः सौन्दर्यलहरी संपूर्णा ॥

YANTRAS
OF
THE SAUNDARYALAHARĪ

In the following pages, *Yantras* relating to the different verses of *Saundaryalaharī* are appended.

A *Yantra* is a diagramatic representation of a *Mantra*, which as a sound-expression conjures up the vision of the Deity, meditated upon.

Meditation in an abstract void is well-nigh impossible, especially in the initial stages and needs tools which can give the senses a perception of the Divine. The pictorial symbolism of the *Yantra*, together with the constant repetition of the *Mantra* enables the mind to concentrate on the object of devotion.

As the devotee concentrates with faith, sincerity and surrender, he feels the presence of the Divine Power in him and gets fortified against the perils and pitfalls, the fears and dangers of life. Earthly accomplishments are of little consequence to the one, whose surrender to the Divine Grace is complete.

The true spiritual aspirant should hence not attach too much importance to the material benefits indicated to accrue in the succeeding pages by the repeated recitation of the various verses, using the *Yantras*. These have been appended mainly to highlight the Tantric aspect of the prayer and its over-all potency.

—**V. K. SUBRAMANIAN**

YANTRAS OF THE INDIVIDUAL VERSES

Verse No. 1

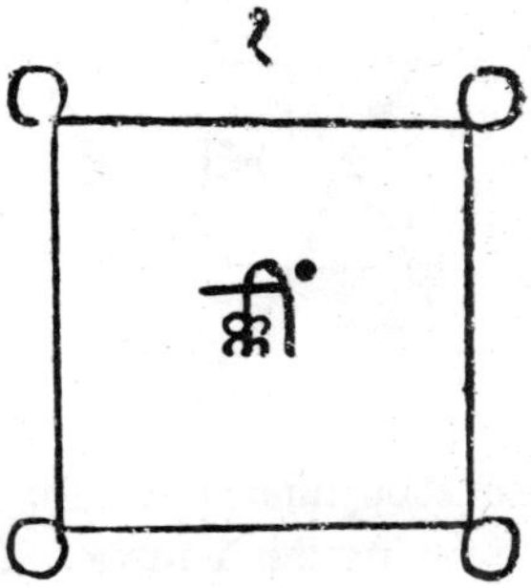

To be recited 1000 times for 12 days.
Material for drawing the Yantra : Gold plate.
Beneficial result : Victory in all tasks undertaken.

Verse No. 2

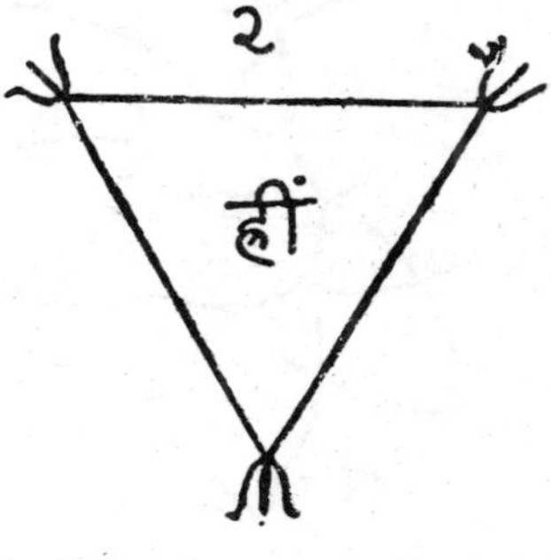

To be repeated 1000 times daily for 55 days.
Material for drawing the Yantra : Gold plate.
Beneficial result : Conquest of nature.

Verse No. 3

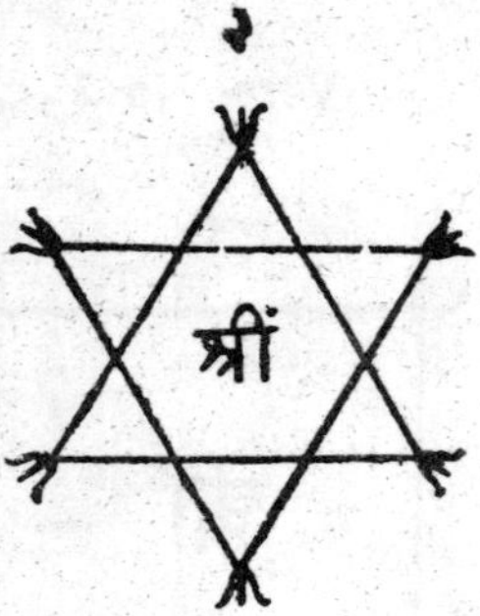

To be repeated 2000 times daily for 54 days.
Material for drawing the Yantra : Gold plate.
Beneficial result : Acquisition of learning and prosperity.

Verse No. 4

To be repeated 3000 times daily for 36 days.
Material for drawing the Yantra : Silver plate.
Beneficial result : Protection from poverty and disease.

Verse No. 5

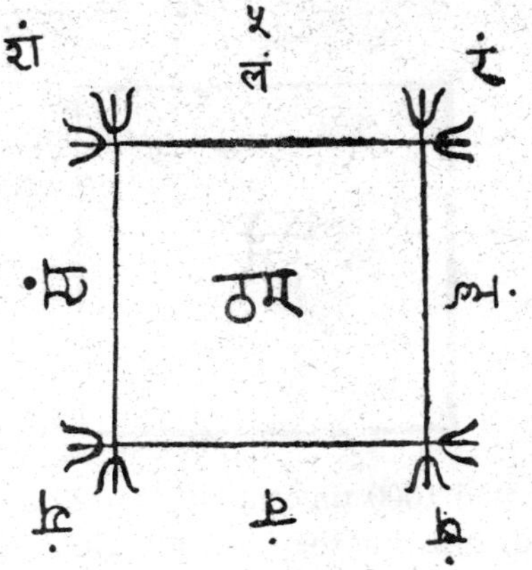

To be repeated 2000 times daily for 8 days.
Material for drawing the Yantra : Copper plate.
Beneficial result : Captivation of all.

Verse No 6

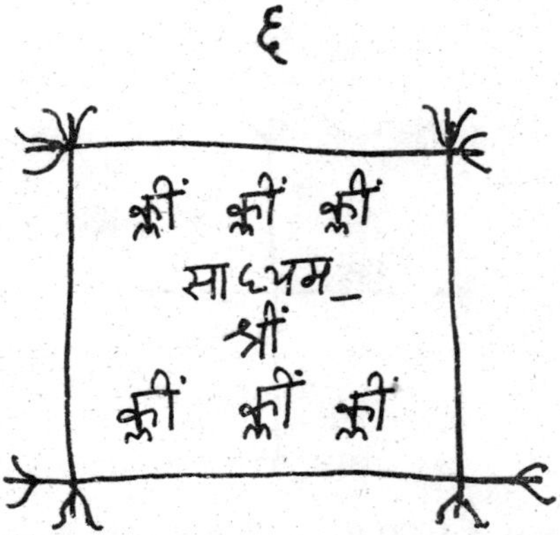

To be repeated 500 times daily for 21 days.
Material for drawing the Yantra : Gold plate.
Beneficial result : Gain of progeny.

Verse No. 7

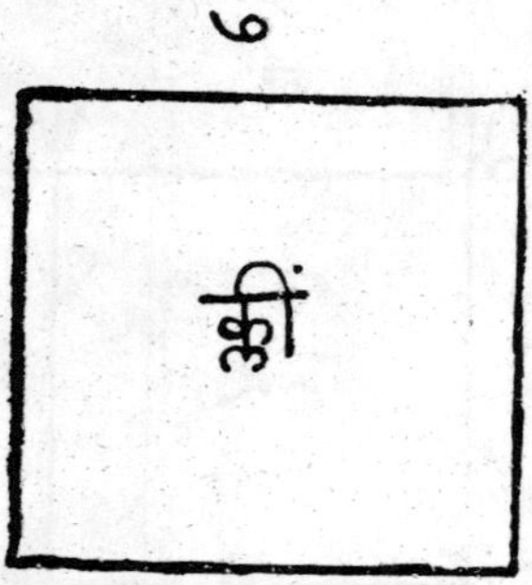

To be repeated 1000 times daily for 12 days.
Material for drawing the Yantra : Gold plate.
Beneficial result : Victory over enemies.

Verse No. 8

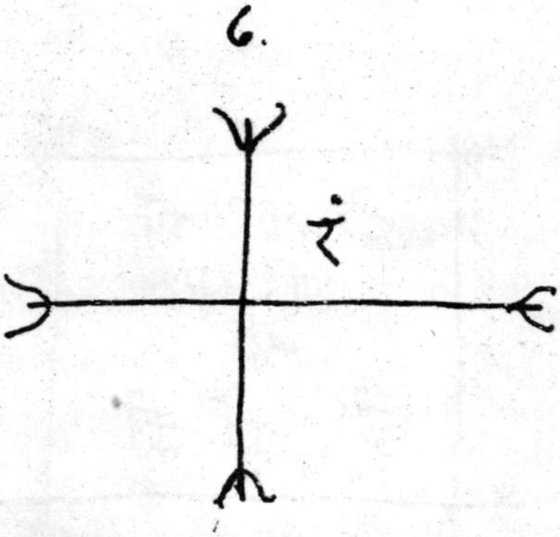

To be repeated 1000 times daily for 12 days.
Material for drawing the Yantra : Red sandal paste.
Beneficial result : Liberation from shackles, success in tasks undertaken.

Verse No. 9

९

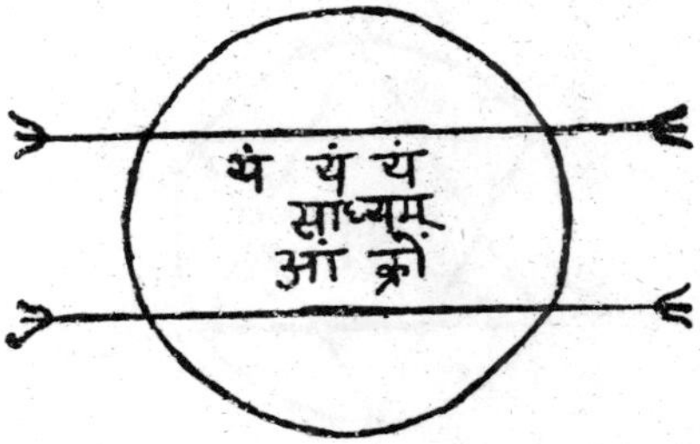

To be repeated 1000 times daily for 45 days.

Material for drawing the Yantra : Gold plate and smeared with civet.

Beneficial result : Mastery over the five elements.

Verse No. 10

१0

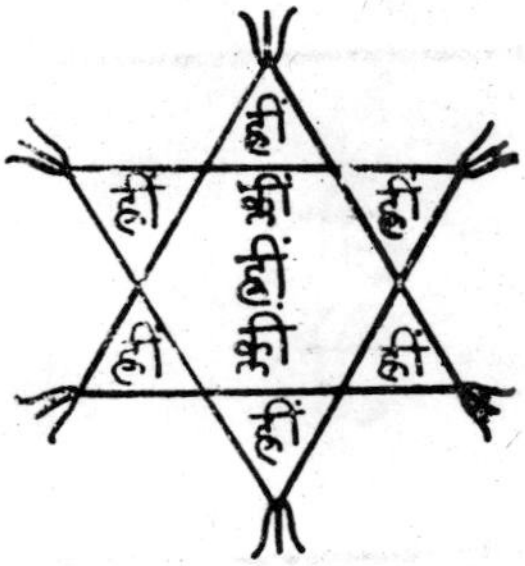

To be repeated 1000 times daily for 6 days.

Material for drawing the Yantra : Gold plate and worn with a red silk thread.

Beneficial result : Increase of sexual vigour.

Verse No. 11

११

To be repeated 1000 times daily for 8 days.
Material for drawing the Yantra : Gold plate.
Beneficial result : Fertility.

Verse No. 12

१२

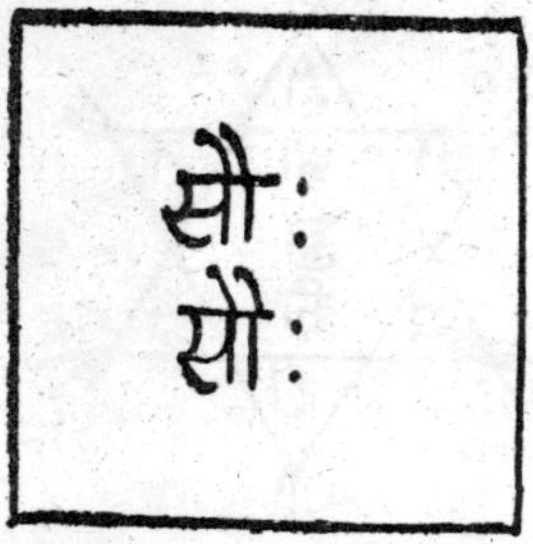

To be repeated 1000 times daily for 45 days.
Material for drawing the Yantra : Water and the water drunk.
Beneficial result : Poetic eloquence.

Verse No. 13

१३

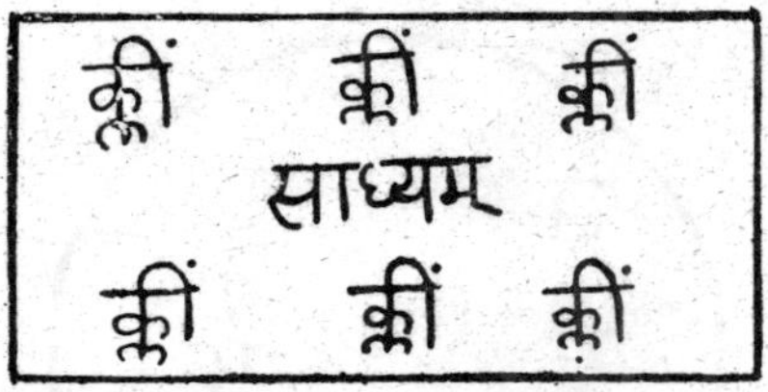

To be repeated 1000 times daily for 6 days.
Material for drawing the Yantra : Gold or Lead plate.
Beneficial result : Power to attract women.

Verse No. 14

१४

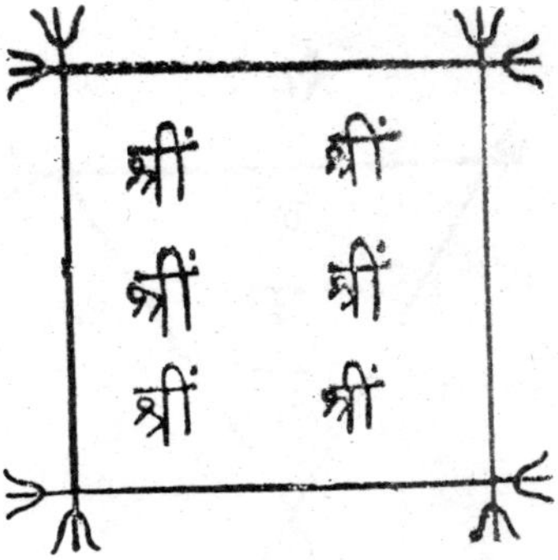

To be repeated 1000 times for 45 days.
Material for drawing the Yantra : Gold plate.
Beneficial result : Prevention of epidemics and famines.

Verse No. 15

१५

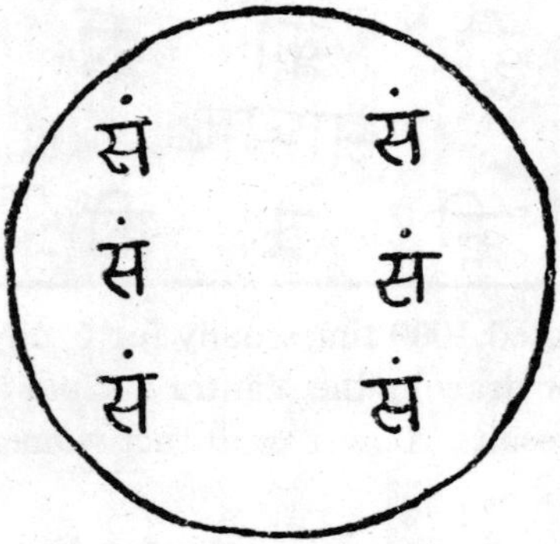

To be repeated 1000 times for 41 days.
Material for drawing the Yantra : Water and the water drunk.
Beneficial result : Knowledge and poetic skill.

Verse No. 16

१६

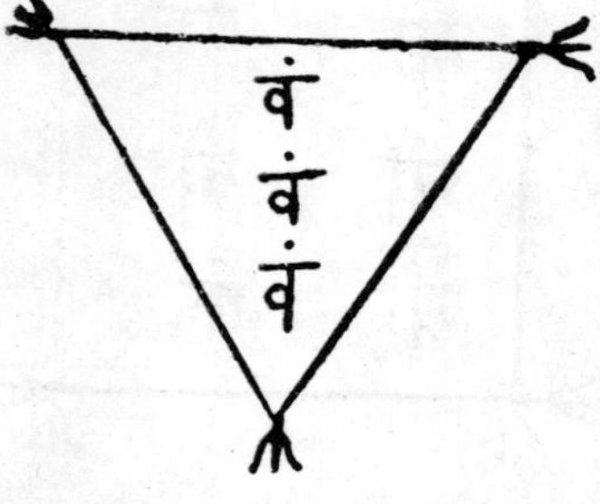

To be repeated 1000 times daily for 41 days.
Material for drawing the Yantra : Gold plate.
Beneficial result : Knowledge of scriptures and sciences.

Verse No. 17

१७

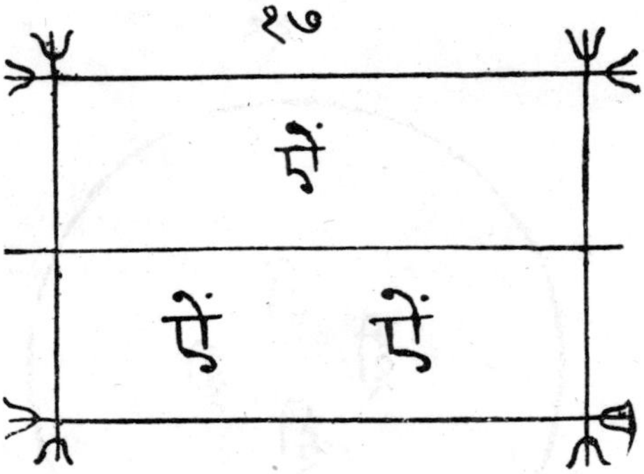

To be repeated 1000 times daily for 45 days.

Material for drawing the Yantra : Gold plate.

Beneficial result : Comprehensive Knowledge of all arts and sciences.

Verse No. 18

१८

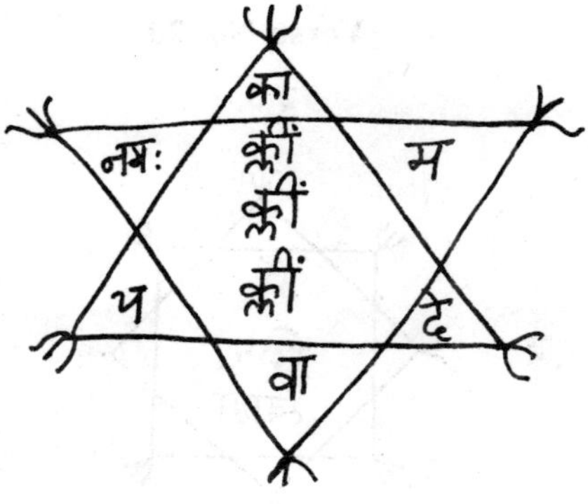

To be repeated 1000 times daily for 45 days.

Material for drawing the Yantra : Gold plate.

Beneficial result : Power to captivate women and artistic skills.

Verse No. 19

१९

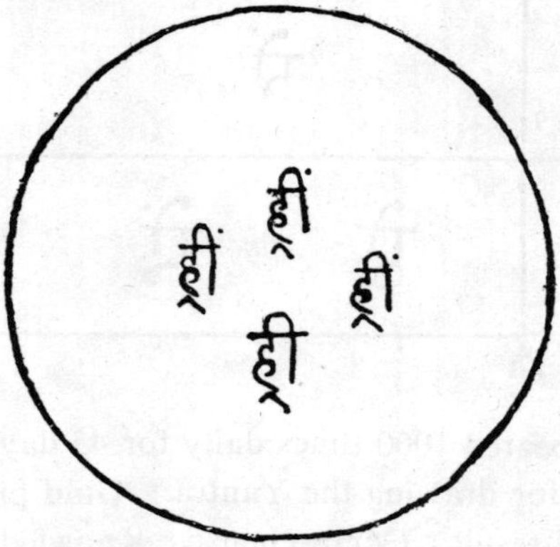

To be repeated 1000 times daily for 25 days.

Material for drawing the Yantra : Gold plate.

Beneficial result : Power to captivate women, animals, demons and rulers.

Verse No. 20

२०

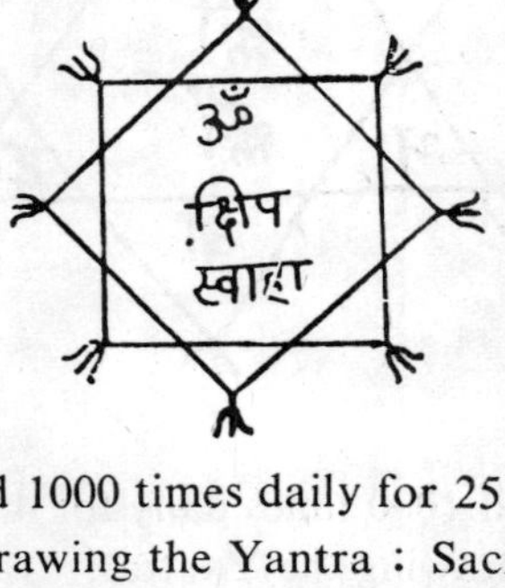

To be repeated 1000 times daily for 25 days.

Material for drawing the Yantra : Sacred ashes or water.

Beneficial result : Power to destroy the effects of poisoning and immunity from poisons.

Verse No. 21

२१

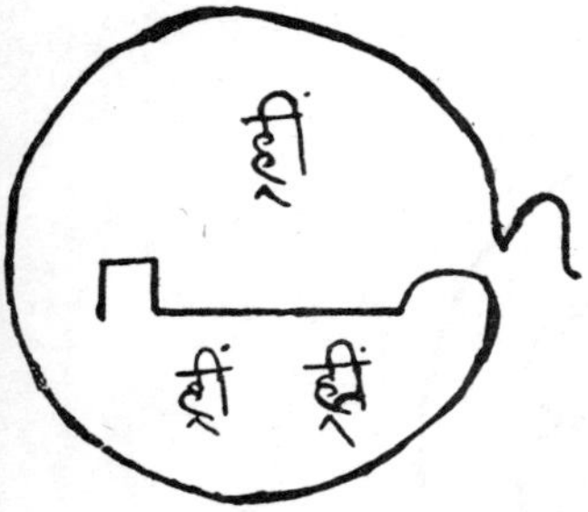

To be repeated 1000 times daily for 11 days.

Material for drawing the Yantra : Gold or silver plate.

Beneficial result : Power to destroy enmity and anger and win over all.

Verse No. 22

२२

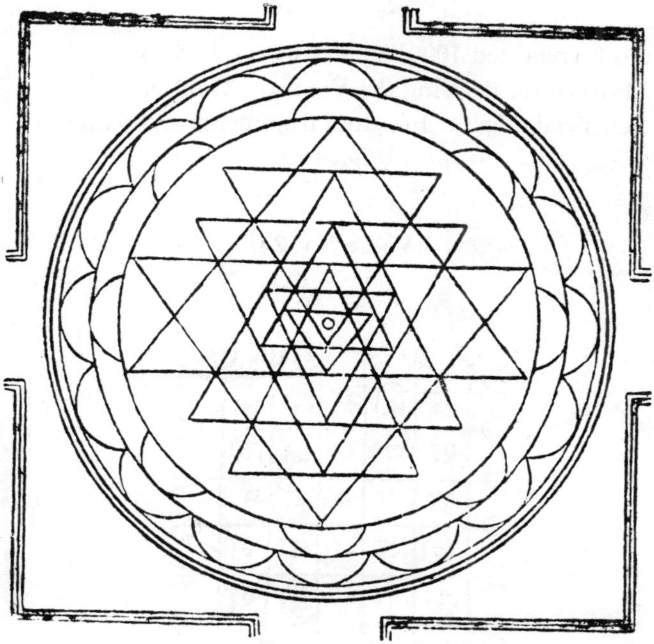

To be repeated 1000 times daily for 45 days.

Material for drawing the Yantra : Gold plate and worshipped at holy places.

Beneficial result : Fulfilment of all desires, ever increasing prosperity, acquisition of empires.

Verse No. 23

२३

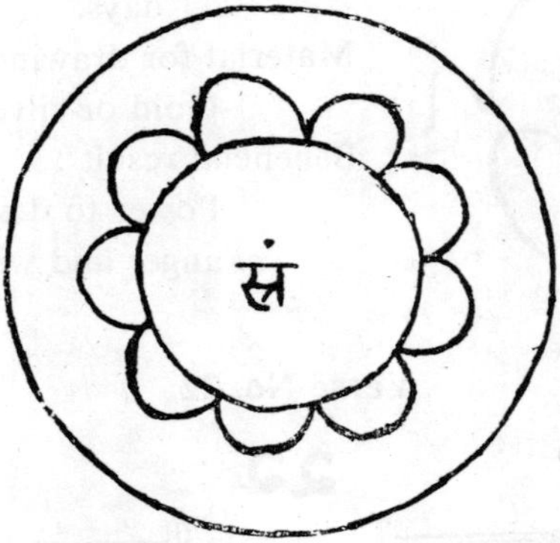

To be repeated 1000 times daily for 45 days.
Material for drawing the Yantra : Gold plate.
Beneficial result : Freedom from debts and dangers.

Verse No. 24

२४

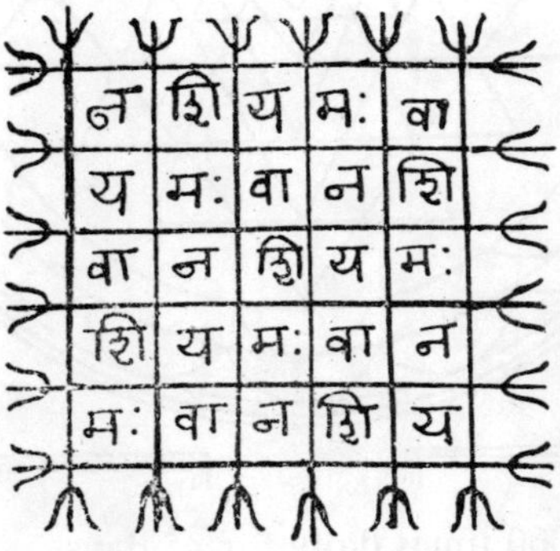

To be repeated 1000 times daily for 20 days.
Material for drawing the Yantra : Gold plate.
Beneficial result : Removal of all evil afflictions.

Verse No. 25

२५

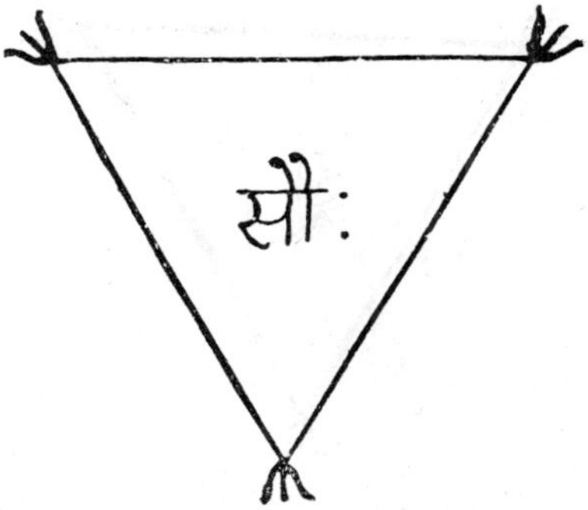

To be repeated 1000 times daily for 45 days.
Material for drawing the Yantra : Gold plate.
Beneficial result : Advancement in professional career.

Verse No. 26

२६

To be repeated 1000 times daily for 6 days.
Material for drawing the Yantra : Gold plate.
Beneficial result ; Destruction of enemies.

Verse No. 27

२७

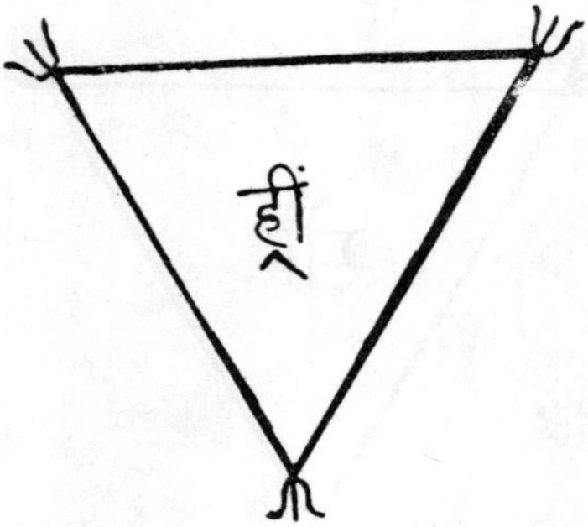

To be repeated 1000 times daily for 45 days.
Material for drawing the Yantra : Gold plate.
Beneficial result : Self-realisation and vision of the Divine.

Verse No. 28

२८

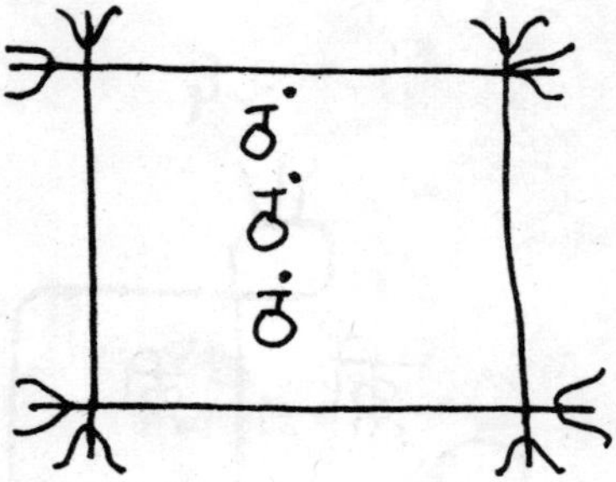

To be repeated 1000 times daily for 45 days.
Material for drawing the Yantra : Gold plate.
Beneficial result : Protection against unforeseen death.

Verse No. 29

२९

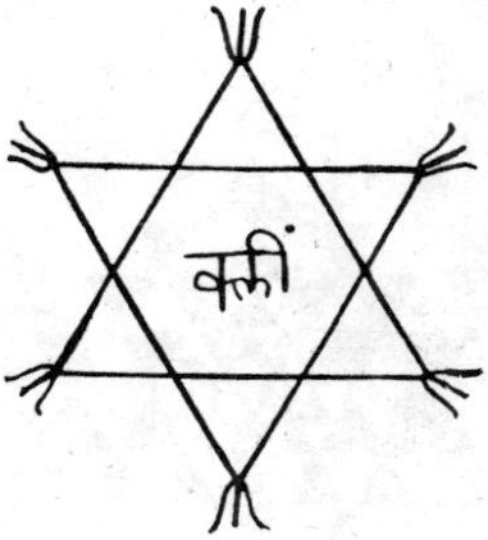

To be repeated 1000 times daily for 45 days.
Material for drawing the Yantra : Gold plate.
Beneficial result : Conversion of wicked enemies into good friends.

Verse No. 30

३०

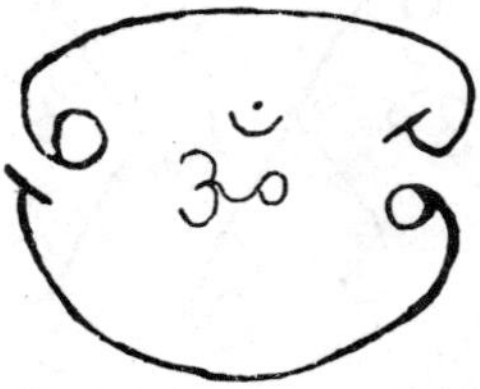

To be repeated 1000 times daily for 96 days.
Material for drawing the Yantra : Gold plate.
Beneficial result : Acquisition of supernatural powers.

Verse No. 31

३१

To be repeated 1000 times daily for 45 days.

Material for drawing the Yantra : Gold plate.

Beneficial result : Power to captivate everyone and all-round prosperity.

Verse No. 32

३२

To be repeated 1000 times daily for 45 days.

Material for drawing the Yantra : Gold plate.

Beneficial result : Knowledge of all sciences and commercial success.

Verse No. 33

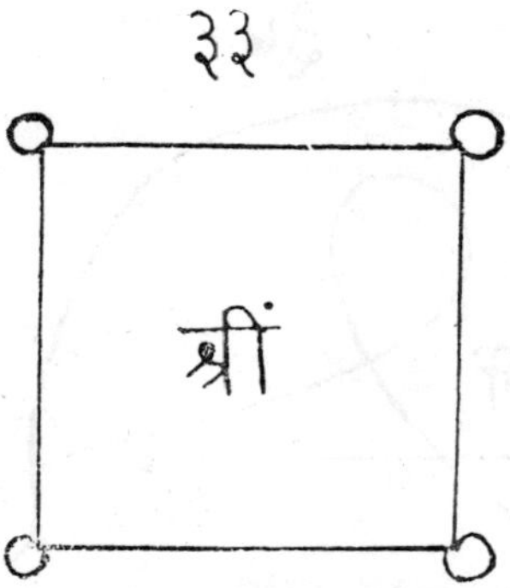

To be repeated 1000 times daily for 45 days.
Material for drawing the Yantra : Gold plate.
Beneficial result : Multiplication of riches.

Verse No. 34

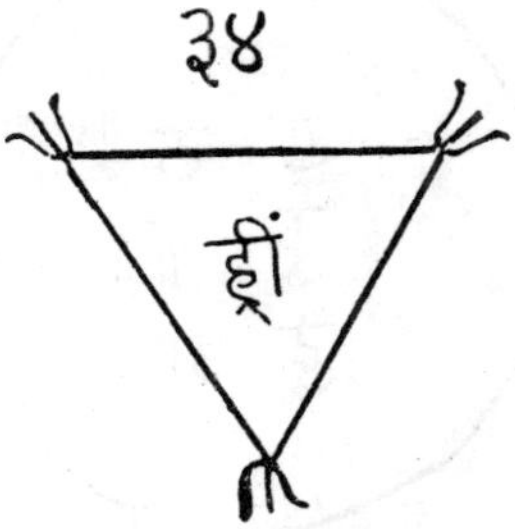

To be repeated 1000 times daily for 45 days.
Material for drawing the Yantra : Gold plate.
Beneficial result : Great intellectual power.

Verse No. 35

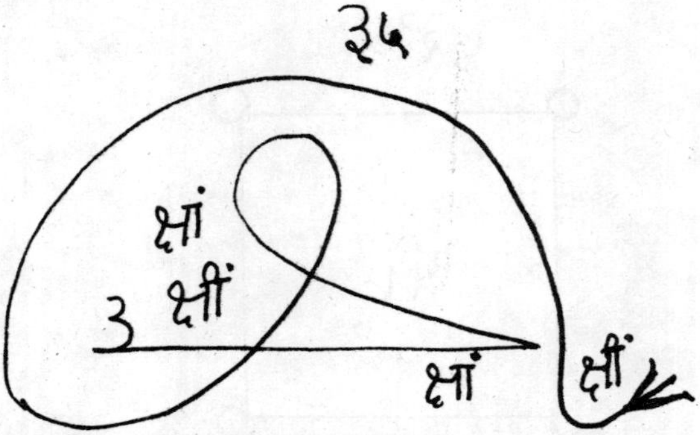

To be repeated 1000 times daily for 45 days.
Material for drawing the Yantra : Gold plate.
Beneficial result : Immunity from wasting diseases.

Verse No 36

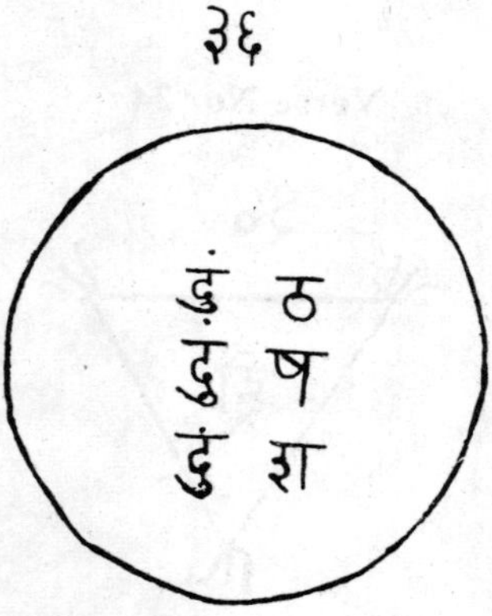

To be repeated 1000 times daily for 45 days.
Material for drawing the Yantra : Gold plate.
Beneficial result ; Elimination of all afflictions.

Verse No. 37

३७

To be repeated 5000 times daily for 45 days.
Material for drawing the Yantra : Gold plate.
Beneficial result : Protection from evil influences.

Verse No. 38

३८

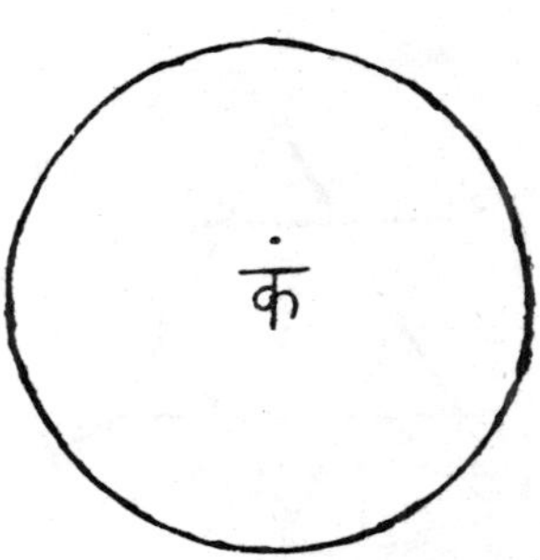

To be repeated 5000 times daily for 45 days.
Material for drawing the Yantra : Gold plate.
Beneficial result : Removal of childhood afflictions.

Verse No. 39

३९

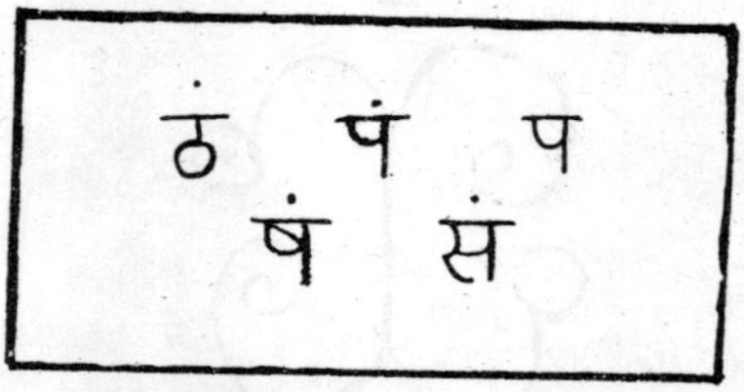

To be repeated 108 times daily for 12 days.
Material for drawing the Yantra : Gold plate.
Beneficial result : Prevention of nightmares.

Verse No. 40

४०

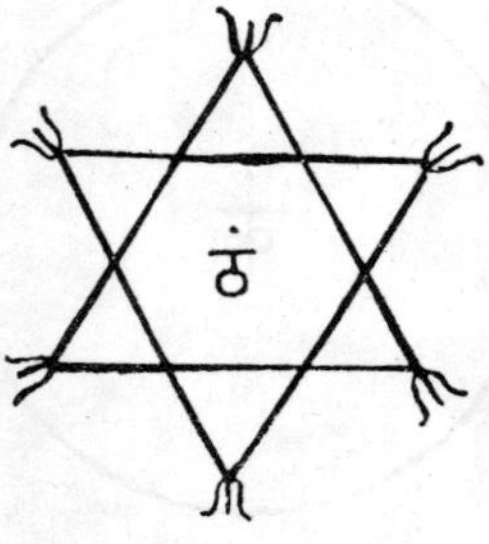

To be repeated 1000 times daily for 45 days.
Material for drawing the Yantra : Gold plate.
Beneficial result : Desired vision in dreams.

Verse No. 41

४१

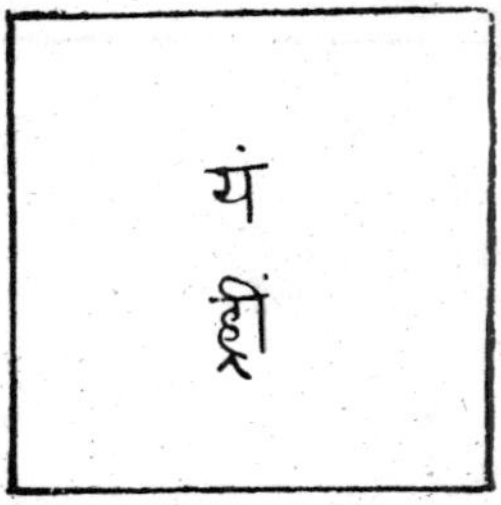

To be repeated 4000 times daily for 30 days.
Material for drawing the Yantra : Gold plate.
Beneficial result : Elimination of all stomach disorders.

Verse No. 42

४२

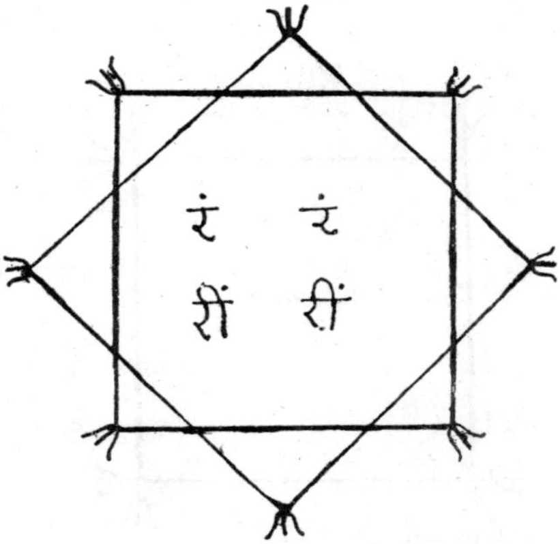

To be repeated 1000 times daily for 45 days.
Material for drawing the Yantra : Gold plate.
Beneficial result : Cure of dropsy.

Verse No. 43

४३

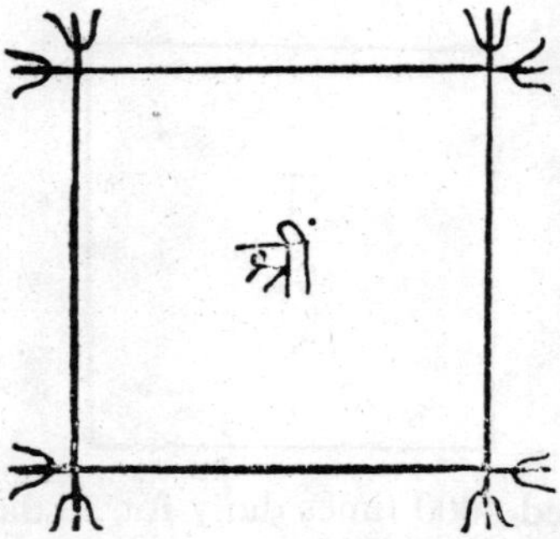

To be repeated 1000 times daily for 45 days.

Material for drawing the Yantra : Gold plate and worn as ring.

Beneficial result : Captivation of all and victory in all projects.

Verse No. 44

४४

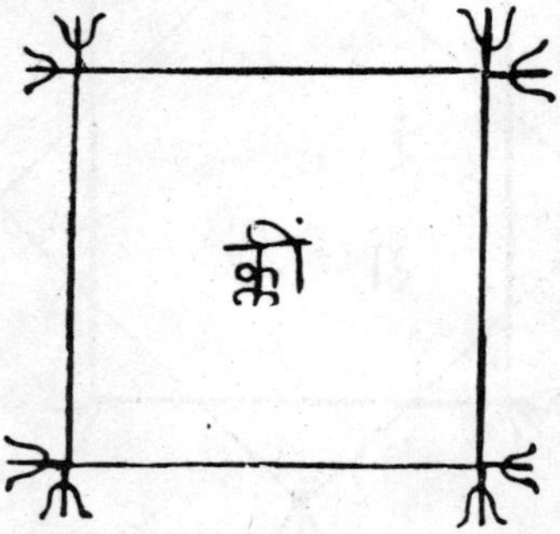

To be repeated 1000 times daily for 12 days.

Material for drawing the Yantra : Gold plate.

Beneficial result : Immunity from all diseases.

Verse No. 45

४५

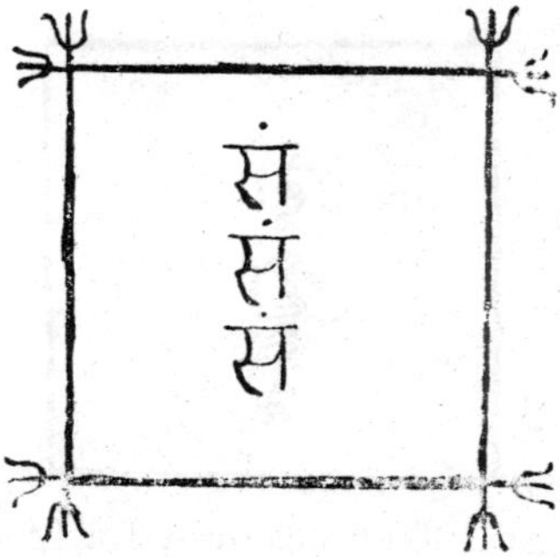

To be repeated 1000 times daily for 45 days.
Material for drawing the Yantra : Gold plate.
Beneficial result : Eloquence.

Verse No. 46

४६

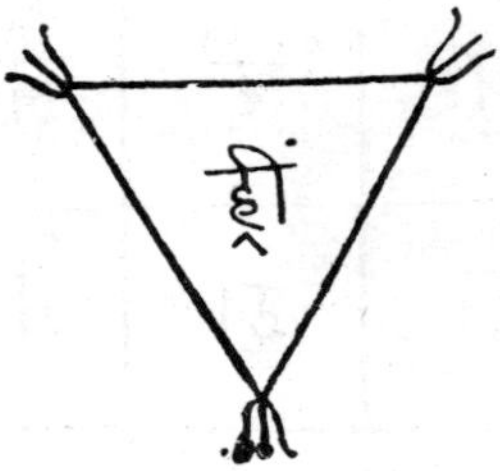

To be repeated 1000 times daily for 45 days.
Material for drawing the Yantra : Gold plate.
Beneficial result : Union with husband and birth of progeny.

Verse No. 47

४७

To be repeated 1000 times daily for 25 days.
Material for drawing the Yantra : Gold plate.
Beneficial result : Power to attract gods and men.

Verse No. 48

४८

बु	शु	च
गु	र	कु
रा	श	के

To be repeated 1000 times daily for 9 days.
Material for drawing the Yantra : Gold plate.
Beneficial result : Power to mitigate the evil influences of planets.

Verse No. 49

४९

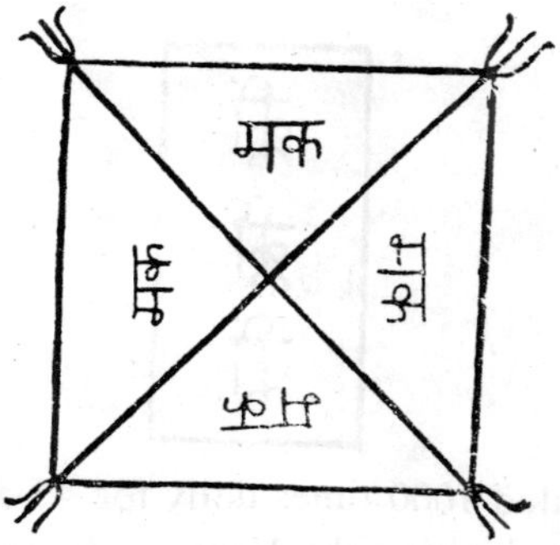

To be repeated 1000 times daily for 10 days.

Material for drawing the Yantra : Turmeric powder, which, after recital, is to be fried on fire, mixed with oil and spread on the palm of a green-eyed boy.

Beneficial result : Location of hidden treasure.

Verse No. 50

५०

To be repeated 1000 times daily for 5 days.

Material for drawing the Yantra : Gold plate or water.

Beneficial result : Immunity from pox.

Verse No. 51

५१

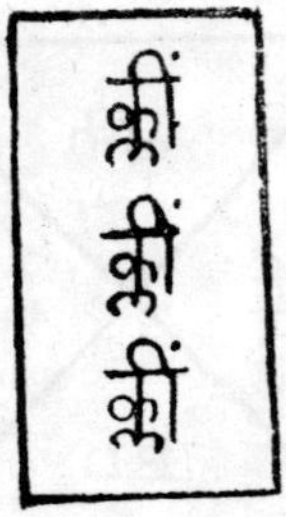

To be repeated 1000 times daily for 45 days.
Material for drawing the Yantra : Gold plate or sandal-paste.
Beneficial result : Power to hypnotise all.

Verse No. 52

५२

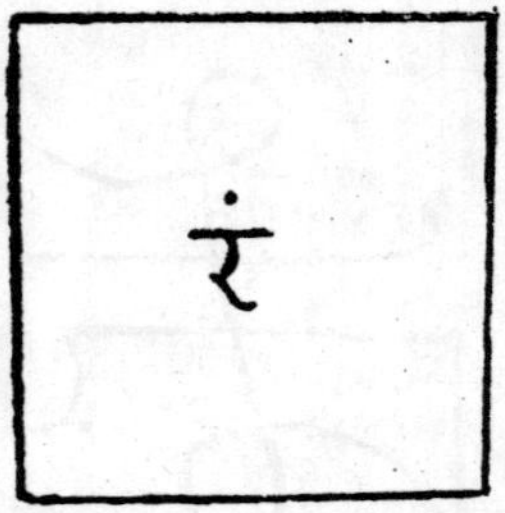

To be repeated 1000 times daily for 45 days.
Material for drawing the Yantra : Gold plate.
Beneficial result : Cure of all diseases relating to eyes and ears.

Verse No. 53

५३

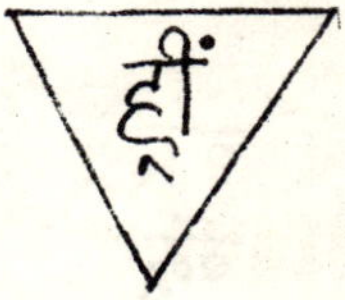

To be repeated 1000 times daily for 45 days.

Material for drawing the Yantra : Gold plate and kept under a lamp.

Beneficial result : Accomplishment of tasks.

Verse No. 54

५४

To be repeated 1000 times daily for 45 days.

Material for drawing the Yantra : Gold plate.

Beneficial result : Cure of gynaecological diseases.

Verse No. 55

५५

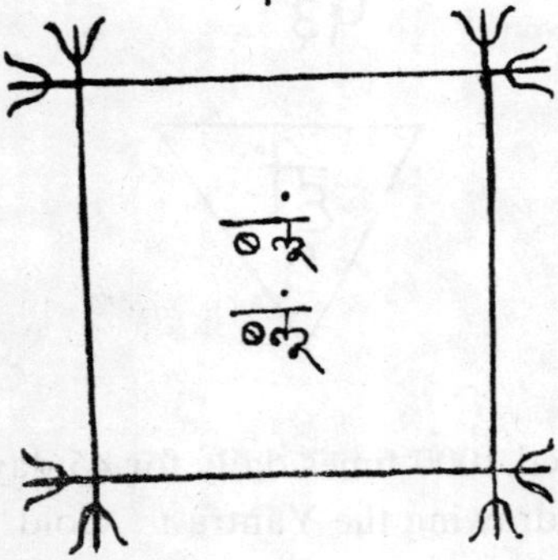

To be repeated 2500 times daily for 45 days.
Material for drawing the Yantra : Gold plate.
Beneficial result : Destruction of enemies.

Verse No. 56

५६

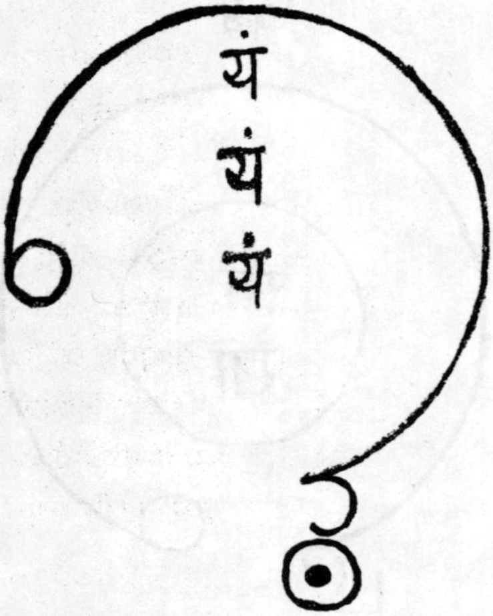

To be repeated 20,000 times for 45 days.
Material for drawing the Yantra : Gold plate.
Beneficial result : Liberation from shackles.

Verse No. 57

५७

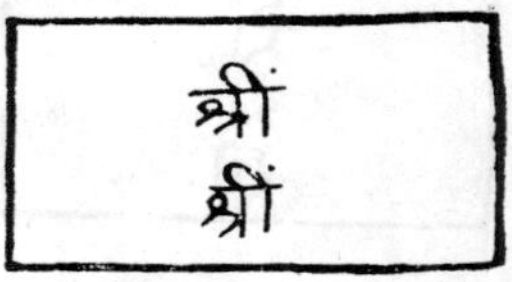

To be repeated 25000 times daily for 6 days.
Material for drawing the Yantra : Gold plate.
Beneficial result : Attainment of all-round Prosperity.

Verse No. 58

५८

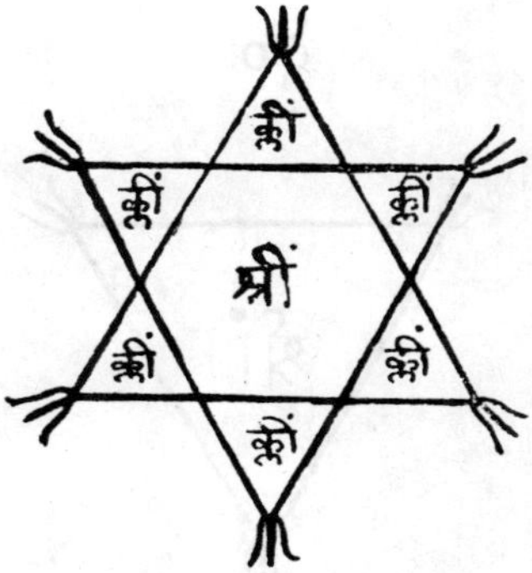

To be repeated 5000 times daily for 45 days.
Material for drawing the Yantra : Saffron powder.
Beneficial result : Power to captivate all, immunity from all diseases.

Verse No. 59

५९

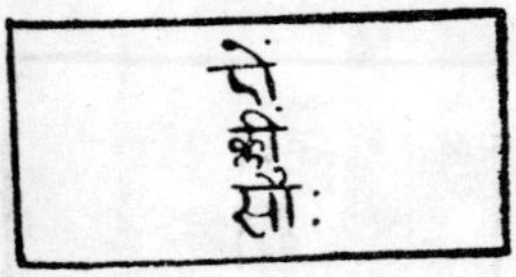

To be repeated 25000 times for 3 days.
Material for drawing the Yantra : Gold plate.
Beneficial result : Power to attract men and women.

Verse No. 60

६०.

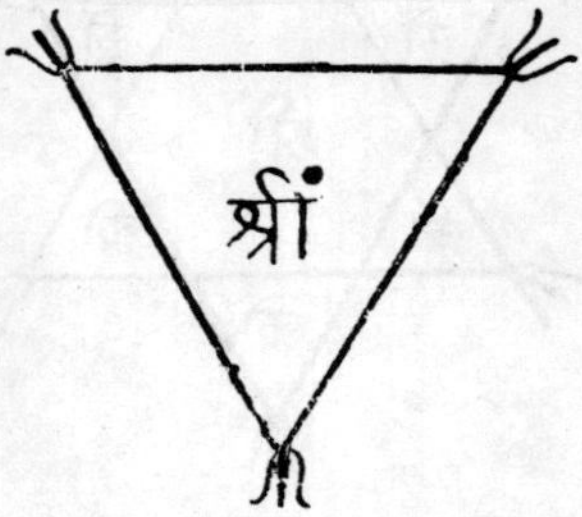

To be repeated 1000 times daily for 45 days.
Material for drawing the Yantra : Gold plate.
Beneficial result : Acquisition of all knowledge.

Verse No. 61

६१

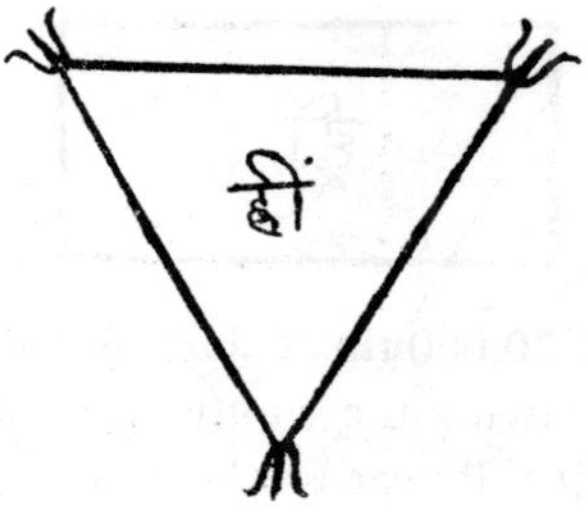

To be repeated 12000 times for 8 days.
Material for drawing the Yantra : Gold plate.
Beneficial result : Success in all tasks undertaken.

Verse No. 62

६२

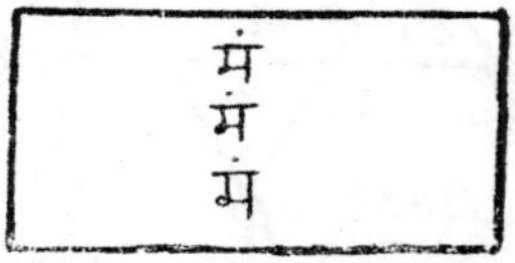

To be repeated 1000 times daily for 8 days.
Material for drawing the Yantra : Gold plate.
Beneficial result : Sweet sleep for insomniacs.

Verse No. 63

६३

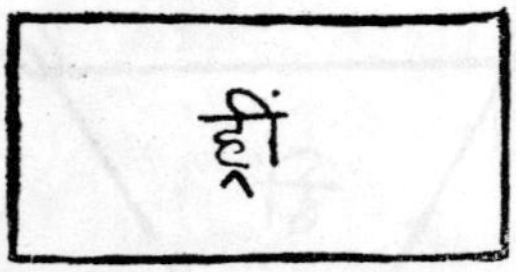

To be repeated 30,000 times daily for 30 days.
Material for drawing the Yantra : Gold plate.
Beneficial result : Power to charm everyone.

Verse No. 64

६४

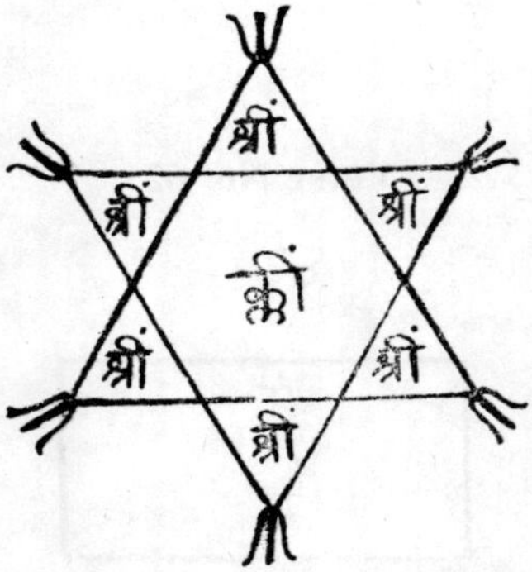

To be repeated 25000 times daily for 18 days.
Material for drawing the Yantra : Saffron powder.
Beneficial result : Power to charm everyone.

Verse No. 65

६५

To be repeated 1000 times daily for 45 days.
Material for drawing the Yantra : Gold plate.
Beneficial result : Victory on all fronts.

Verse No. 66

६६

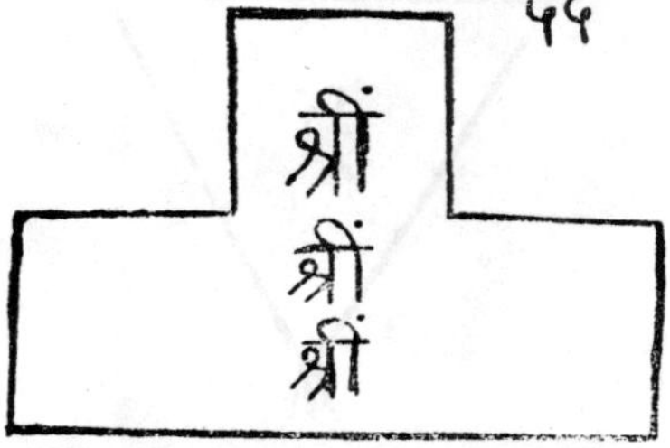

To be repeated 5000 times daily for 3 days.
Material for drawing the Yantra : Gold plate.
Beneficial result : Proficiency in music.

Verse No. 67

६७

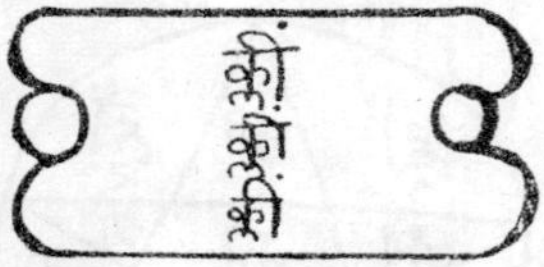

To be repeated 1000 times daily for 45 days.
Material for drawing the Yantra : Gold plate.
Beneficial result : Development of deep bonds of love in couples.

Verse No. 68

६८

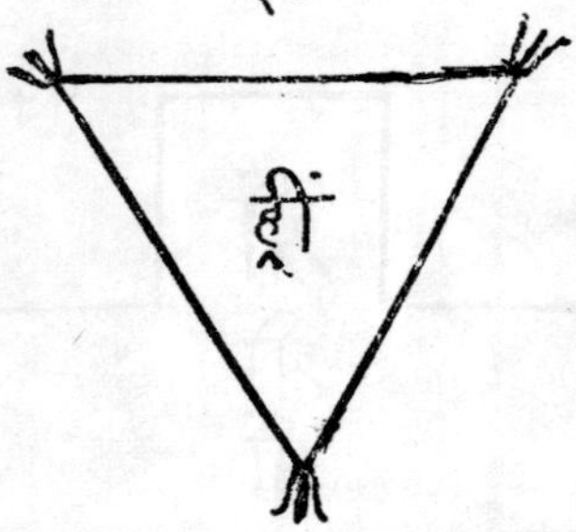

To be repeated 1000 times daily for 45 days.
Material for drawing the Yantra : Saffron powder.
Beneficial result : Power to captivate rulers.

Verse No. 69

६९

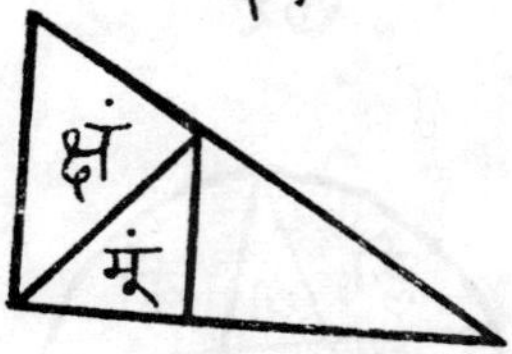

To be repeated 1000 times daily for 45 days.
Material for drawing the Yantra : Gold plate.
Beneficial result : Success in all tasks.

Verse No. 70

७०.

To be repeated 1000 times daily for 45 days.
Material for drawing the Yantra : Gold plate.
Beneficial result : Power to conquer men.

Verse No. 71

७१

To be repeated 12000 times daily for 45 days.
Material for drawing the Yantra : Gold plate.
Beneficial result : Power to conquer female friends.

Verse No. 72

७२

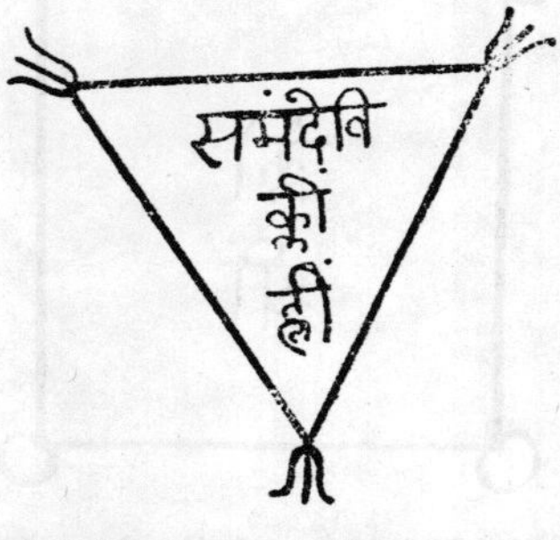

To be repeated 1000 times daily for 45 days.
Material for drawing the Yantra : Gold plate.
Beneficial result : Fear-free, trouble-free travel.

Verse No. 73

७३

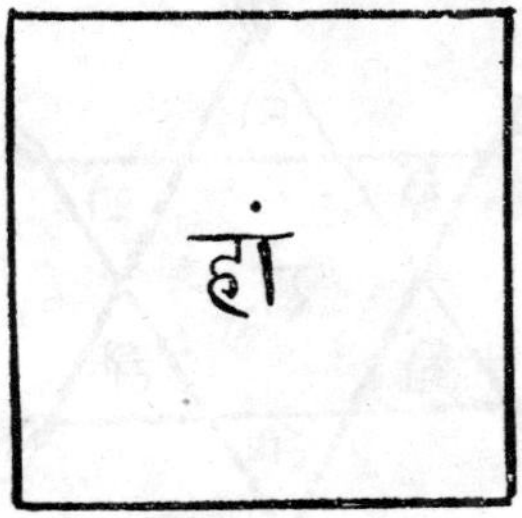

To be repeated 1000 times daily for 8 days.
Material for drawing the Yantra : Gold plate.
Beneficial result : Abundance of milk in mothers.

Verse No. 74

७४

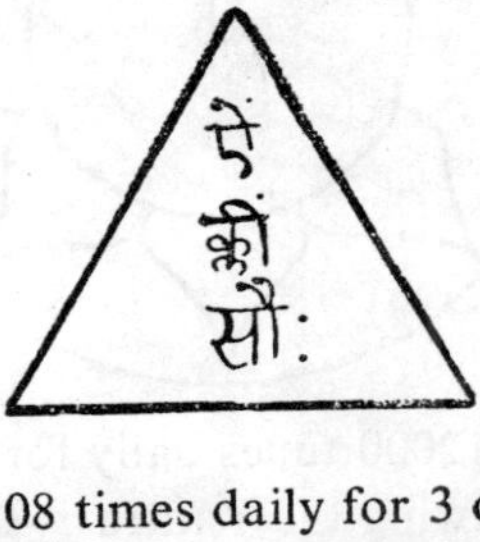

To be repeated 108 times daily for 3 days.
Material for drawing the Yantra : Gold plate.
Beneficial result : Fame.

Verse No. 75

७५

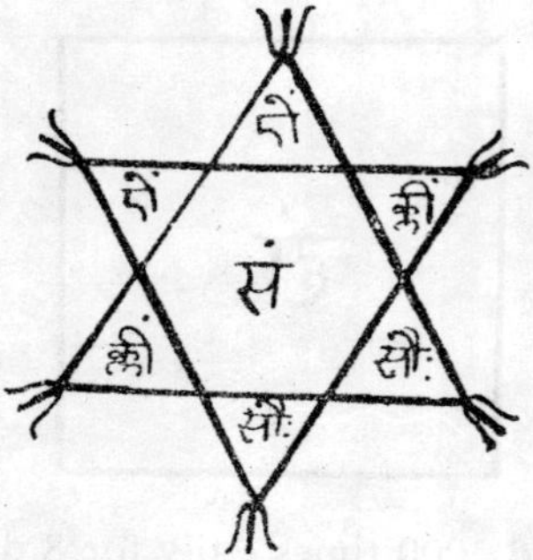

To be repeated 1000 times daily for 3 days.
Material for drawing the Yantra : Gold plate.
Beneficial result : Poetic skill.

Verse No. 76

७६

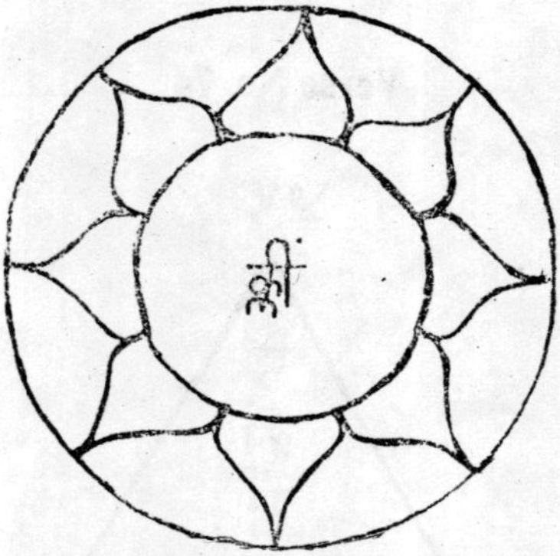

To be repeated 12000 times daily for 8 days
Material for drawing the Yantra : Gold plate.
Beneficial result : Power to charm all and win victory in all tasks undertaken.

Verse No. 77

७७

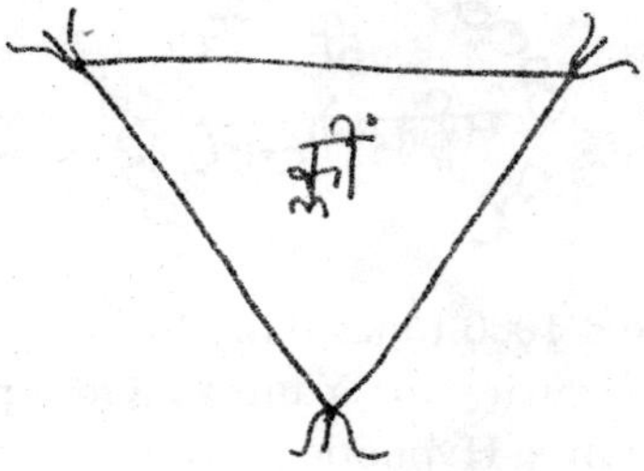

To be repeated 2000 times daily for 15 days.
Material for drawing the Yantra : Gold plate.
Beneficial result : Advancement in career.

Verse No. 78

७८

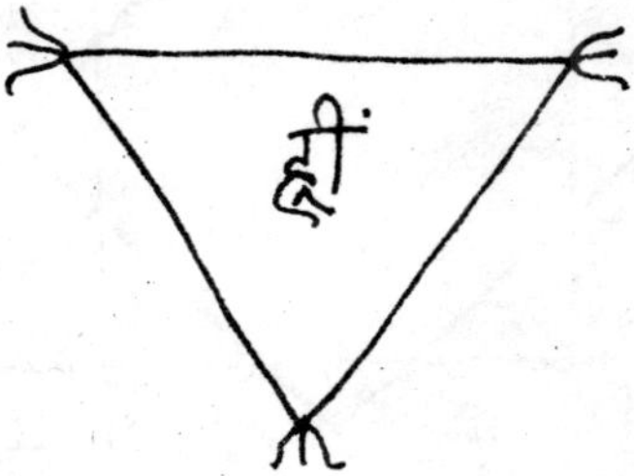

To be repeated 108 times daily for 45 days.
Material for drawing the Yantra : Sandal-paste.
Beneficial result : Victory in tasks undertaken.

Verse No. 79

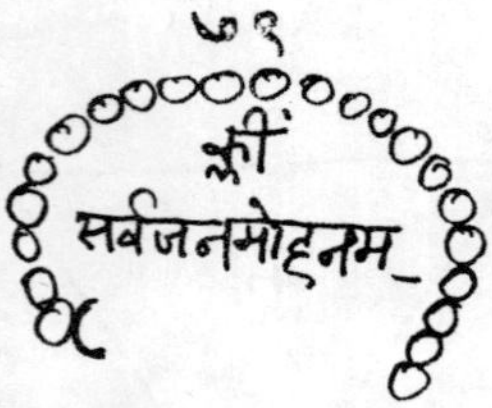

To be repeated 1000 times daily for 45 days.
Material for drawing the Yantra : Gold plate.
Beneficial result : Hypnotic powers.

Verse No 80

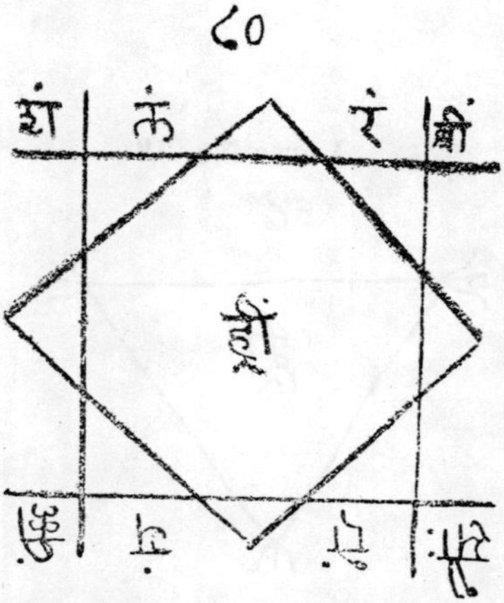

To be repeated 1000 times daily for 45 days.
Material for drawing the Yantra : Gold plate.
Beneficial result : Magical powers.

Verse No. 81

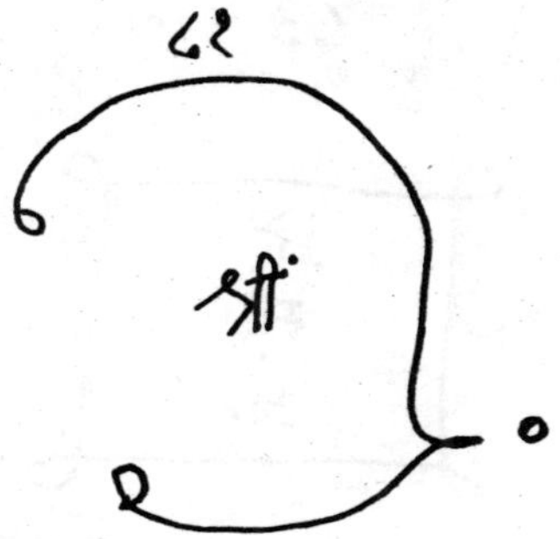

To be repeated 1000 times daily for 16 days.
Material for drawing the Yantra : Gold plate.
Beneficial result : Control over fire.

Verse No. 82

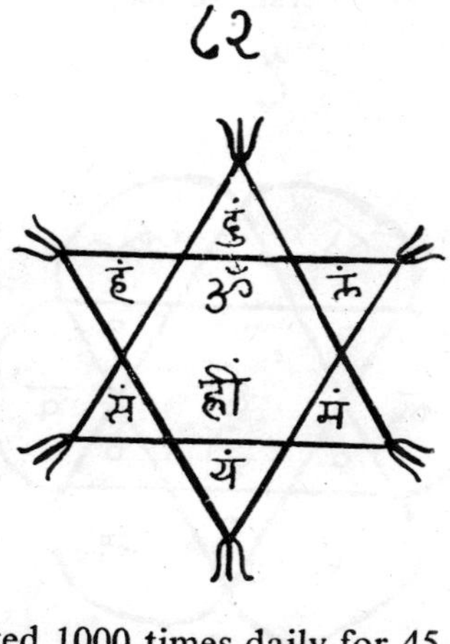

To be repeated 1000 times daily for 45 days.
Material for drawing the Yantra : Birch-tree-leaf and worn with footwear.
Beneficial result : Control over water.

Verse No. 83

८३

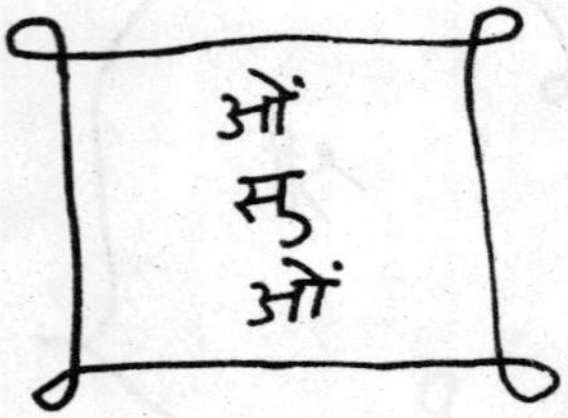

To be repeated 1000 times daily for 12 days.
Material for drawing the Yantra : Gold plate.
Beneficial result : Control over elephants, horses and armies.

Verse No. 84

८४

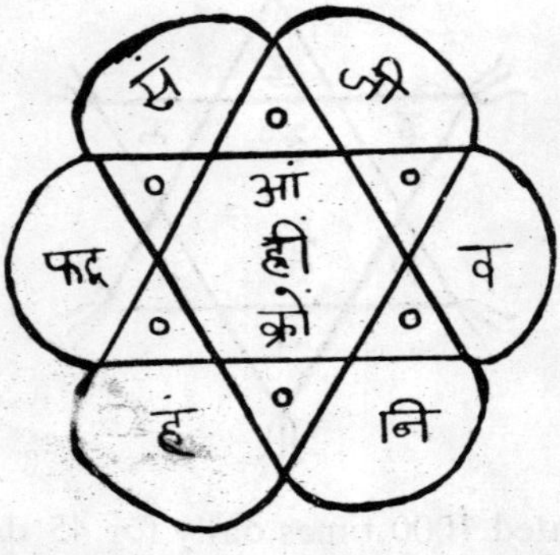

To be repeated 1000 times daily for 1 year.
Material for drawing the Yantra : Gold plate.
Beneficial result : Power to enter other bodies.

Verse No. 85

८५

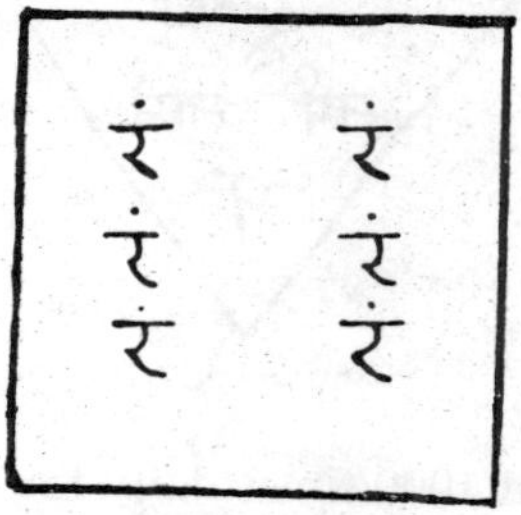

To be repeated 1000 times daily for 12 days.
Material for drawing the Yantra : Gold plate.
Beneficial result : Power to remove evil spirits.

Verse No. 86

८६

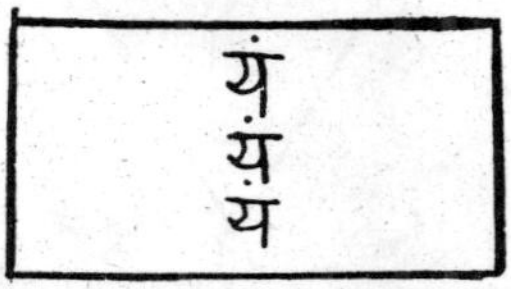

To be repeated 1000 times daily for 21 days.
Material for drawing the Yantra : Gold plate.
Beneficial result : Removal of evil afflictions.

Verse No. 87

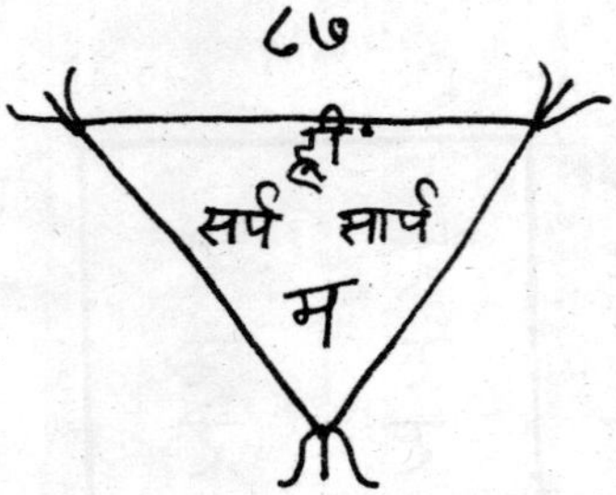

To be repeated 1000 times daily for 16 days.
Material for drawing the Yantra : Gold plate.
Beneficial result : Control over serpents.

Verse No. 88

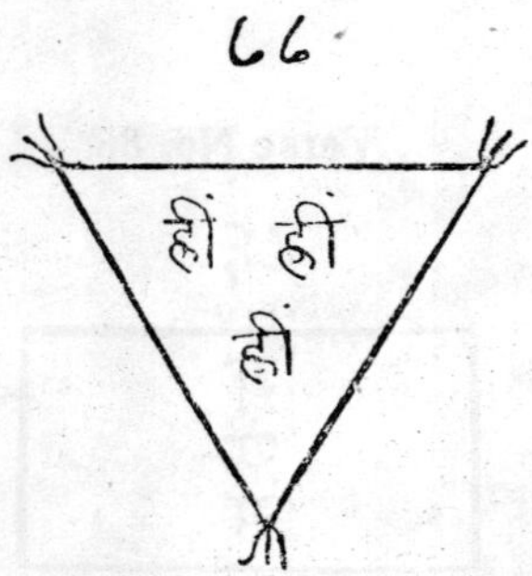

To be repeated 1000 times daily for 15 days.
Material for drawing the Yantra : Gold plate.
Beneficial result : Control over animals.

Verse No. 89

८९

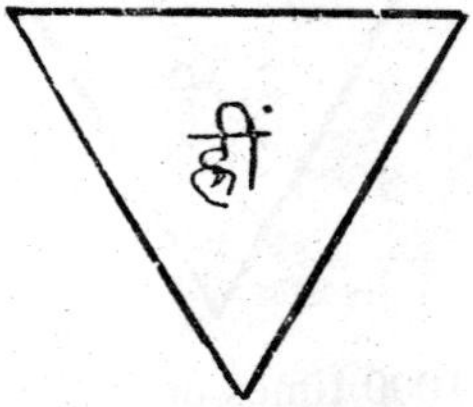

To be repeated 1000 times daily for 30 days.
Material for drawing the Yantra : Gold plate.
Beneficial result : Elimination of all diseases.

Verse No. 90

९०

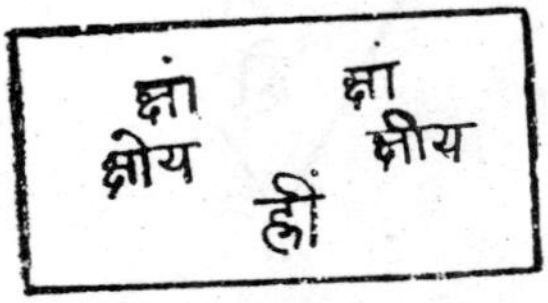

To be repeated 1000 times daily for 30 days.
Material for drawing the Yantra : Gold plate.
Beneficial result : Power to combat mean practices.

Verse No. 91

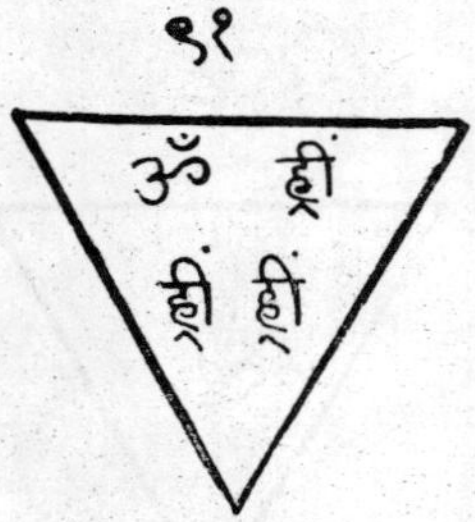

To be repeated 1000 times daily for 25 days.
Material for drawing the Yantra : Gold plate.
Beneficial result : Acquisition of land, property and riches.

Verse No. 92

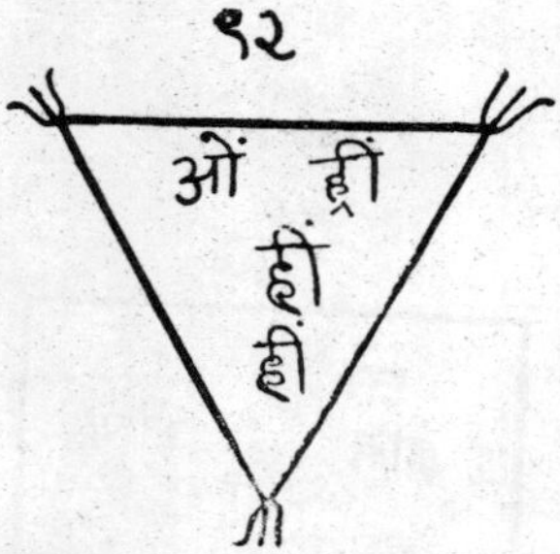

To be repeated 4000 times daily for 30 days.
Material for drawing the Yantra : Gold plate.
Beneficial result : Accrual of kingdoms.

Verse No. 93

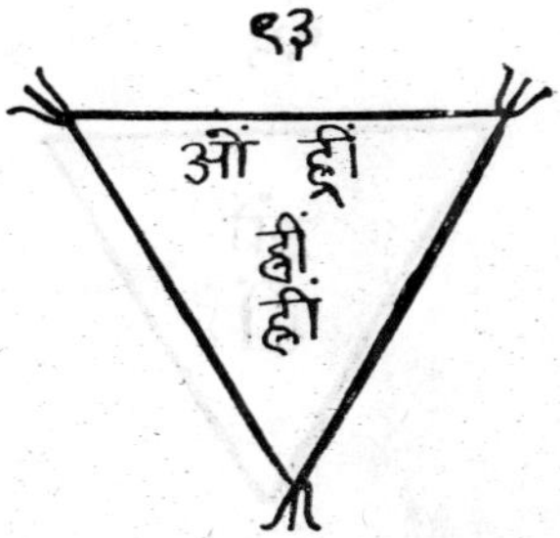

To be repeated 2000 times daily for 25 days.
Material for drawing the Yantra : Gold plate.
Beneficial result : Fulfilment of all desires.

Verse No. 94

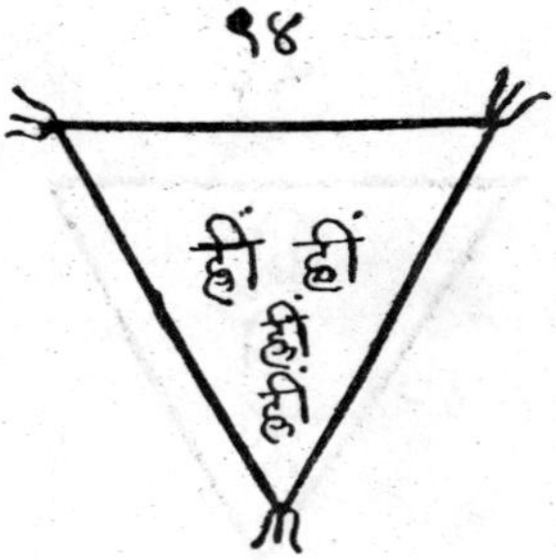

To be repeated 1000 times daily for 45 days.
Material for drawing the Yantra : Gold plate.
Beneficial result : Attainment of objectives.

Verse No. 95

९५

To be repeated 108 times daily for 45 days.
Material for drawing the Yantra : Gold plate.
Beneficial result : Healing of all wounds.

Verse No. 96

९६

To be repeated 1000 times daily for 45 days.
Material for drawing the Yantra : Gold plate.
Beneficial result : Knowledge of arts.

Verse No 97

९७

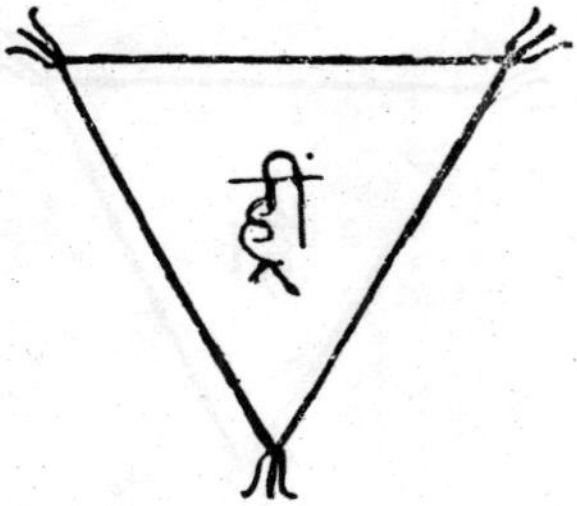

To be repeated 1000 times daily for 8 days.
Material for drawing the Yantra : Gold plate.
Beneficial result : Strong physical health.

Verse No. 98

९८

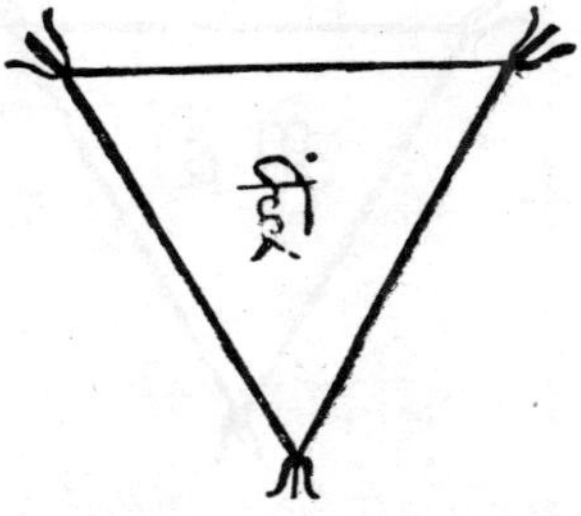

To be repeated 1000 times daily for 30 days.
Material for drawing the Yantra : Gold plate.
Beneficial result : Sexual happiness.

Verse No. 99

९९

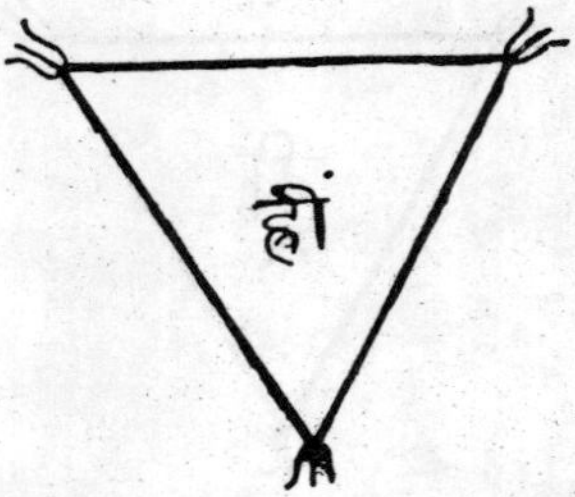

To be repeated 1000 times daily for 16 days.
Material for drawing the Yantra : Gold plate
Beneficial result : Endowment of valour.

Verse No. 100

१००

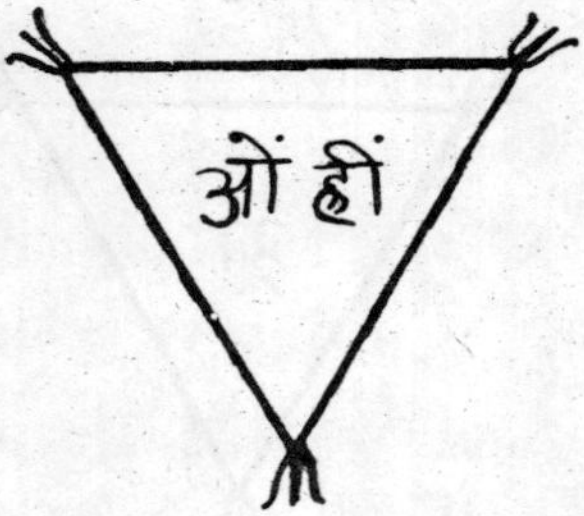

To be repeated 1000 times daily for 16 days.
Material for drawing the Yantra : Gold plate.
Beneficial result : Achievement of all ideals.

PĀDA INDEX
सौन्दर्यलहर्यन्तर्गत-श्लोक-पादसूची

अतः शेषः शेषीत्य् 34 *c*
अतस्ते विस्तीर्णो 81 *c*
अतस्ते शीतांशोर् 63 *c*
अतस्तेषां शिक्षां 91 *c*
अतस्त्वद्द्रोगेन 94 *c*
अतस्त्वामाराध्यां 1 *c*
अनेनायं धन्यो 57 *c*
अपाङ्गव्यासङ्गो 58 *d*
अपाङ्गात्ते लब्ध्वा 6 *d*
अमन्दं सौन्दर्य° 90 *b*
अमी हृल्लेखाभिस् 32 *c*
अमुञ्चन्तौ दृष्ट्वा 50 *c*
अमू ते वक्षोजा° 73 *a*
अरालं ते पाली° 58 *a*
अराला केशेषु 93 *a*
अरालैः स्वाभाव्याद् 45 *a*
अवन्ती दृष्टिस्ते 49 *c*
अवाप्य स्वां भूमिं 10 *c*
अविद्यानामन्तस्° 3 *a*
अविश्रान्तं पत्युर् 64 *a*
असूयत्यत्यन्तं 85 *c*
असूयासंसर्गाद् 50 *d*
असौ नासावंशस् 61 *a*
अहः सूते सव्यं 48 *a*
इति स्तोतुं वाञ्छन् 22 *b*
इमे नेत्रे गोत्रा° 52 *c*
इयं च श्रीर्बद्ध° 56 *c*
उभाभ्यामूरुभ्याम् 82 *b*
उभाभ्यामेताभ्याम् 41 *c*
कटाक्षव्याक्षेप° 50 *b*
कठोरे कोटीरे 29 *b*
कथंकारं ब्रूमस् 67 *d*
कथं नीतं सद्भिः 88 *b*
कथं वा बाहुभ्यां 88*c*
कदा काले मातः 98 *a*
कदा धत्ते वाणी° 98 *d*
कयाचिद्वा साम्यं 71 *c*
करग्राह्यं शंभोर् 67 *c*
कराग्रेण स्पृष्टं 67 *a*
कराणां ते कान्ति 71 *b*
करालं यत्क्ष्वेलं 28 *c*
करीन्द्राणां शुण्डान् 82 *a*
कलङ्कः कस्तूरी 94 *a*
कलत्रं वैधात्रं 96 *a*
कलाभिः कर्पूरैर् 94 *b*
कलावालं कुण्डं 78 *b*
कवीनां प्रौढानाम् 75 *d*
कवीनां सन्दर्भ° 50 *a*
कवीन्द्राः कल्पन्ते 12 *b*
कवीन्द्राणां चेतः° 16 *a*
कषन्तौ दोर्मूले 80 *b*
किमाश्चर्यं तस्य 30 *c*
किरन्तीमङ्गेभ्यः 20 *a*
किरीटं ते हैमं 42 *b*
किरीटं वैरिञ्चं 29 *a*
कुचाभोगो बिम्बा° 74 *c*
कुचाभ्यामानम्रं 23 *d*
कुचाभ्यामासङ्गः 96 *d*

कुचौ सद्यः स्विद्यत्° 80 *a*
कुमारावद्यापि 73 *d*
कृपाधाराधारा 49 *b*
कृशे मध्ये किंचिज् 77 *b*
क्वणत्काञ्चीदामा 7 *a*
क्षितौ षट्पञ्चाशद् 14 *a*
गतास्ते मञ्चत्वं 92 *a*
गतिः प्रादक्षिण्य° 27 *b*
गते कर्णाभ्यर्णं 52 *a*
गतैर्माणिक्यत्वं 42 *a*
गभीराभिर्वाग्भिर् 16 *d*
गभीरे ते नाभी° 76 *b*
गलद्वेणीबन्धाः 13 *c*
गले रेखास्तिस्रो 69 *a*
गिरामाहुर्देवीं 97 *a*
गिरीशेनोदस्तं 67 *b*
गुरुत्वं विस्तारं 81 *a*
घनस्निग्धश्लक्ष्णं 43 *b*
चकोराणामासीद् 63 *b*
चतुःषष्ट्या तन्त्रैः 31 *a*
चतुर्णां शीर्षाणां 70 *d*
चतुर्भिः श्रीकण्ठैः 11 *a*
चतुर्भिः सौन्दर्यं 70 *b*
चतुश्चक्रं मन्ये 59 *b*
चतुश्चत्वारिंशद् 11 *c*
चमत्कारश्लाघा° 60 *c*
चिदानन्दाकारं 35 *d*
चिरं जीवन्नेव 99 *c*
चिरं ते मध्यस्य 79 *c*
चिरादन्तःशल्यं 86 *c*
च्छलादाचक्षाणां 91 *d*
जगत्त्रातुं शंभोर् 93 *d*
जगत्सूते धाता 24 *a*
जडानां चैतन्य° 3 *b*
जनस्तां जानीते 76 *d*
जपापुष्पच्छाया 64 *b*
जपो जल्पः शिल्पं 27 *a*
जहाति प्रत्यूषे 56 *d*
ज्वरप्लुष्टान् दृष्ट्या 20 *d*
झणत्कारैस्तारैः 60 *d*
तटित्त्वन्तं शक्त्या 40 *a*
तटिल्लेखातन्वीं 21 *a*
तथाप्येकः सर्वं 6 *c*
तथा हि त्वत्पादो° 25 *c*
तथाह्येते नीताः 95 *c*
तदैव त्वं तस्मै 22 *c*
तनीयांसं पांसुं 2 *a*
तनुच्छायाभिस्ते 18 *a*
तनूभूतं व्योम 77 *d*
तनोतु क्षेमं नस् 44 *a*
तपोभिर्दुष्प्रापाम् 12 *d*
तमीडे संवर्तं 39 *b*
तरूणां दिव्यानां 89 *b*
तव ग्रीवा धत्ते 68 *b*
तव त्रातुं भङ्गाद् 80 *c*
तव द्वारोपान्त° 95 *d*
तव श्यामं मेघं 40 *c*
तव स्तन्यं मन्ये 75 *a*
तव स्वाधिष्ठाने 39 *a*
तवाकर्णाकृष्ट° 52 *d*
तवाज्ञाचक्रस्थं 36 *a*
तवाज्ञामालम्ब्य 24 *d*
तवात्मानं मन्ये 34 *b*
तवाधारे मूले 41 *a*
तवापर्णे कर्णे° 56 *a*
तवापाङ्गालोके 13 *b*

तवास्मिन् मन्दार° 90 *c*
तवास्मै द्वन्द्वाय 85 *b*
तवेत्याहुः सन्तो 55 *b*
तवेदं नः खेदं 72 *b*
तिरश्चीनो यत्र 58 *c*
तिरस्कुर्वन्नेतत् 24 *b*
तुरीया कापि त्वं 97 *c*
तुलाकोटिक्वाणैः 86 *d*
तुलामध्यारोढुं 62 *d*
तृतीया ते दृष्टिर् 48 *c*
त्रयाणां ग्रामाणां 69 *d*
त्रयाणां तीर्थानां 54 *d*
त्रयाणां देवानां 25 *a*
त्रिधा नद्धं देवि 80 *d*
त्रियामां वामं ते 48 *b*
त्रिरेखाभिः सार्धं 11 *d*
त्रिलोकीमप्याशु 19 *d*
त्वदन्यः पाणिभ्याम् 4 *a*
त्वदीयं सौन्दर्यं 12 *a*
त्वदीयानां भासां 92 *c*
त्वदीयाभिर्वाग्भिस् 100 *d*
त्वदीये नेत्राभ्यां 47 *b*
त्वदीयैर्माधुर्यैर् 66 *c*
त्वदीयो नेदीयः 61 *b*
त्वदुन्मेषाज्जातं 55 *c*
त्वमापस्त्वं भूमिस् 35 *b*
त्वमेका नैवासि 4 *b*
त्वमेव स्वात्मानं 35 *c*
त्वयारब्धे वक्तुं 66 *b*
त्वया हृत्वा वामं 23 *a*
ददाने दीनेभ्यः 90 *a*
दयामित्रैर्नेत्रैर् 54 *b*
दयार्द्रा या दृष्टिः 39 *d*
दयावत्या दत्तं 75 *c*
दरस्मेरे यस्मिन् 45 *c*
दरिद्राणां चिन्ता° 3 *c*
दरिद्रेभ्यो भद्रां 89 *d*
दवीयांसं दीनं 57 *b*
दिवं सर्वामुर्वीम् 18 *b*
दिवि द्विःषट्त्रिंशन् 14 *c*
दृशा द्राघीयस्या 57 *a*
द्वितीयं तन्मन्ये 46 *b*
द्विषां वृन्दैर्बन्दी° 44 *d*
धनुः पौष्पं मौर्वी 6 *a*
धनुः शौनासीरं 42 *d*
धनुर्बाणान् पाशं 7 *c*
धनुर्मन्ये सव्ये° 47 *c*
धुनोतु ध्वान्तं 43 *a*
ध्रुवं तत्तन्नाम° 49 *d*
न केषामाधत्ते 58 *b*
नखाग्रच्छद्मानः 83 *d*
नखानामुद्योतैर् 71 *a*
नखेभ्यः संत्रस्यन् 70 *c*
नखैर्नाकस्त्रीणां 89 *a*
न चेदेवं देवो 1 *b*
नदः शोणो गङ्गा 54 *c*
न बिम्बं तद्बिम्ब° 62 *c*
नमन्मूर्तेर्नारी° 79 *b*
नमोवाकं ब्रूमो 85 *a*
नरं वर्षीयांसं 13 *a*
नवात्मानं मन्ये 41 *b*
न शंभोस्तन्मूलं 28 *d*
न संदेहस्पन्दो 73 *b*
निजां वीणां वाणी 66 *d*
नितम्बप्राग्भारः 81 *d*
नितम्बादाच्छिद्य 81 *b*

निधायैके नित्ये 33 *b*
निमग्नानां द्रंष्ट्रा 3 *d*
निमज्जन् मज्जीवः 90 *d*
निमेषोन्मेषाभ्यां 55 *a*
निरालोकेऽलोके 36 *d*
निलीयन्ते तोये 56 *b*
निवृत्तैश्चण्डांश° 65 *b*
निशायां निद्राणं 87 *b*
निषङ्गौ जङ्घे ते 83 *b*
निषण्णां षण्णामप्य् 21 *b*
निषेवे नित्ये त्वाम् 30 *b*
निषेवे वर्षन्तं 40 *d*
निसर्गक्षीणस्य 79 *a*
पदं ते कीर्तीनां 88 *a*
पदन्यासक्रीडा° 91 *a*
पयःपारावारः 75 *b*
परं शंभुं वन्दे 36 *b*
पराजेतुं रुद्रं 83 *b*
परानन्दाभिख्यं 99 *d*
परिक्षीणा मध्ये 7 *b*
परित्रातुं शङ्के 55 *d*
परीतं ते वक्त्रं 45 *b*
परीवाहस्रोतः° 44 *b*
पवित्रीकर्तुं नः 54 *a*
पशूनामीशानः 85 *d*
पिबन्ति स्वच्छन्दं 63 *d*
पिबन्तौ तौ यस्माद् 73 *c*
पिबन्त्याः शर्वाणि 60 *b*
पिबेयं विद्यार्थी 98 *b*
पुनः स्रष्टुं देवान् 53 *c*
पुनस्त्वन्निर्बन्धाद् 31 *c*
पुरस्तादास्तां नः 7 *d*
पुरां भेत्तुश्चित्त° 52 *b*
पुरा नारी भूत्वा 5 *b*
पुरारातेरन्तः° 95 *a*
प्रकृत्या मूकानाम् 98 *c*
प्रकृत्या रक्तायास् 62 *a*
प्रकोष्ठे मुष्टौ च 47 *d*
प्रणन्तुं स्तोतुं वा 1 *d*
प्रणम्रेष्वेतेषु 29 *c*
प्रणामः संवेशः 27 *c*
प्रतापव्यामिश्रां 74 *d*
प्रदीपज्वालाभिर् 100 *a*
प्रपञ्चं सिञ्चन्ती 10 *b*
प्रभिन्नाभिः शंभोर् 11 *b*
प्रवक्ष्ये सादृश्यं 62 *b*
फलानि स्वःस्थेभ्यः 89 *c*
बिलद्वारं सिद्धेर् 78 *d*
भजन्ति त्वां चिन्ता° 33 *c*
भजन्ति त्वां धन्याः 8 *d*
भजन्ते ये सन्तः 16 *b*
भजन्ते वर्णास्ते 32 *d*
भजे हंसद्वन्द्वं 38 *b*
भयात्त्रातुं दातुं 4 *c*
भवन्त्यस्य त्रस्यद्° 18 *c*
भवस्याभ्युत्थाने 29 *d*
भवानि त्वं दासे 22 *a*
भवेत्पूजा पूजा 25 *b*
भुजाश्लेषान्नित्यं 68 *a*
भृशं तन्वी मध्ये 93 *c*
भ्रुवौ भुग्ने किंचिद् 47 *a*
मणिद्वीपे नीपो° 8 *b*
मधुक्षीरद्राक्षा° 15 *d*
मनस्त्वं व्योम त्वं 35 *a*
मनोऽपि भ्रूमध्ये 9 *c*
ममाप्येतौ मातः 84 *b*
मयूखास्तेषामप्य् 14 *d*
महादेवं हित्वा 96 *c*
महान्तः पश्यन्तो 21 *d*
महापद्माटव्यां 21 *c*

महामाया विश्वं 97 *d*
महावीरो मारः 59 *d*
महासंवर्ताग्निर् 30 *d*
महासंहारेऽस्मिन् 26 *d*
महीं मूलाधारे 9 *a*
मुकुन्दब्रह्मेन्द्र° 22 *d*
मुखं बिन्दुं कृत्वा 19 *a*
मुनीनामप्यन्तः 5 *d*
मृणालीमृद्वीनां 70 *a*
मृणालीलालित्यं 68 *d*
मृषा कृत्वा गोत्र° 86 *a*
यदग्रासीनायाः 64 *c*
यदग्रे दृश्यन्ते 83 *c*
यदादत्ते दोषाद् 38 *d*
यदादाय न्यस्तं 88 *d*
यदालापादष्टा° 38 *c*
यदालोके लोकान् 39 *c*
यदालोकौत्सुक्याद् 12 *c*
यदालोक्याशङ्का° 72 *c*
यदि क्रीडल्लक्ष्मी° 71 *d*
यदीयं सौरभ्यं 43 *c*
यदेतत्कालिन्दी° 77 *a*
यदेतत्त्वद्रूपं 23 *c*
यमाराध्यन् भक्त्या 36 *c*
यमारुह्य द्रुह्यत्य् 59 *c*
ययोः कान्त्या यान्त्याः 37 *c*
ययोः पद्यं पाथः 84 *c*
ययोर्लाक्षालक्ष्मीर् 84 *d*
रजः सत्त्वं बिभ्रत् 53 *d*
रणे जित्वा दैत्यान् 65 *a*
रतेः पातिव्रत्यं 99 *b*
रतेर्लीलागारं 78 *c*
ललाटं लावण्य° 46 *a*
ललाटे भर्तारं 86 *b*
वचोभिर्वाग्देवी° 17 *d*
वने वा हर्म्ये वा 57 *d*
वरं लक्ष्मीपात्रं 87 *c*
वरत्रासत्राण° 15 *b*
वशिन्याद्याभिस्त्वां 17 *b*
वसन्तः सामन्तो 6 *b*
वसन्त्यस्मिन्मन्ये 43 *d*
वहत्यम्ब स्तम्बे° 74 *a*
वहत्येनं शौरिः 2 *c*
वहन्ती सिन्दूरं 44 *c*
वहन्त्यन्तर्मुक्ताः 61 *c*
वितन्द्री माहेन्द्री 26 *c*
विधिज्ञे जानुभ्यां 82 *d*
विधिर्भूयो भूयो 94 *d*
विधूतान्तर्ध्वान्ता 37 *d*
विनाशं कीनाशो 26 *b*
विपञ्च्या गायन्ती 66 *a*
विपद्यन्ते विश्वे 28 *b*
विपर्यासन्यासाद् 46 *c*
विभक्तत्रैवर्ण्यं 53 *a*
विभाति त्वन्नेत्र° 53 *b*
विमर्दादन्योन्यं 77 *c*
विराजन्ते नाना° 69 *c*
विरिञ्चिः पञ्चत्वं 26 *a*
विरिञ्चिः संचिन्वन् 2 *b*
विरिञ्चिप्रेयस्यास् 16 *c*
विलीयन्ते मातस् 65 *d*
विवाहव्यानद्ध° 69 *b*
विशाखेन्द्रोपेन्द्रैः 65 *c*
विशाला कल्याणी 49 *a*
विशुद्धौ ते शुद्ध° 37 *a*
शरज्ज्योत्स्नाशुद्धां 15 *a*
शरण्ये लोकानां 4 *d*
शरीरं त्वं शंभोः 34 *a*
शरीरार्धं शंभोर् 23 *b*
शरीरी शृङ्गारो 92 *d*

शिरीषाभा चित्ते 93 *b*
शिवं सेवे देवीम् 37 *b*
शिवः शक्तिः कामः 32 *a*
शिवः शक्त्या युक्तो 1 *a*
शिवः स्वच्छच्छाया° 92 *b*
शिवाकारे मञ्चे 8 *c*
शिवाग्नौ जुह्वन्तः 33 *d*
शिवे शृङ्गारार्द्रा 51 *a*
श्रियो देव्याः को वा 96 *a*
श्रुतीनां मूर्धानो 84 *a*
स कर्ता काव्यानां 17 *c*
सकृन्न त्वा नत्वा 15 *c*
सखीषु स्मेरा ते 51 *d*
सदापूर्वः सर्वं 24 *c*
सनाथाभ्यां जज्ञे 41 *d*
स नीडेयच्छाया° 42 *c*
सपर्यापर्यायस् 27 *d*
सपर्यामर्यादा 95 *b*
समं देवि स्कन्द° 72 *a*
समाधत्ते सन्ध्यां 48 *d*
समारब्धां मुक्ता° 74 *b*
समावस्थास्थेम्नो 79 *d*
समुत्तस्थौ तस्माद् 76 *c*
समुन्मीलत्संवित्° 38 *a*
समृद्धया यत्तासां 61 *d*
सरस्वत्याः सूक्तीर् 60 *a*
सरस्वत्या मूर्तिः 64 *d*
सरस्वत्या लक्ष्म्या 99 *a*
सरोजं त्वत्पादौ 87 *d*
सरोषा गङ्गायां 51 *b*
सवित्रीभिर्वाचां 17 *a*
स सद्यः संक्षोभं 19 *c*
स सर्पाणां दर्पं 20 *c*
सहस्रारे पद्मे 9 *d*
सहोर्वश्या वश्याः 18 *d*
सुगन्धौ माद्यन्ति 45 *d*
सुधाधारासारैश् 10 *a*
सुधामप्यास्वाद्य 28 *a*
सुधालेपस्यूतिः 46 *d*
सुधासिन्धोर्मध्ये 8 *a*
सुधासूतेश्चन्द्रो° 100 *b*
सुवृत्ताभ्यां पत्युः 82 *c*
स्खलन्तस्ते खेलं 91 *b*
स्थितं स्वाधिष्ठाने 9 *b*
स्थितः संबन्धो वां 34 *d*
स्थितस्तत्तत्सिद्धि° 31 *b*
स्थिता ह्येते शश्वन् 25 *d*
स्थिरो गङ्गावर्तः 78 *a*
स्फुरद्गण्डाभोग° 59 *a*
स्फुरन्नानारत्ना° 40 *b*
स्मरं योनिं लक्ष्मीं 33 *a*
स्मरोऽपि त्वां नत्वा 5 *c*
स्मरो हंसः शक्रस् 32 *b*
स्मितज्योत्स्नाजालं 63 *a*
स्वकीयैरम्भोभिः 100 *c*
स्वकुम्भौ हेरम्बः 72 *d*
स्वतः श्वेता काला° 68 *c*
स्वतन्त्रं ते तन्त्रं 31 *d*
स्वदेहोद्भूताभिर् 30 *a*
स्वमात्मानं कृत्वा 10 *d*
हठात्त्रुटयत्काञ्च्यो 13 *d*
हरः संक्षुद्यैनं 2 *d*
हरक्रोधज्वाला° 76 *a*
हरार्धं ध्यायेद्यो 19 *b*
हराहिभ्यो भीता 51 *c*
हरिस्त्वामाराध्य 5 *a*
हरेः पत्नीं पद्मां 97 *b*
हिमानीहन्तव्यं 87 *a*
हुताशे द्वाषष्टिश् 14 *b*
हृदि त्वामाधत्ते 20 *b*